Pilates

Fitness training for body and soul

Antje Korte

BARNES
& NOBLE

NEW YORK

© 2004 GRÄFE UND UNZER VERLAG GmbH, Munich.

This edition published by Barnes & Noble, Inc., by arrangement with GRÄFE UND UNZER VERLAG GmbH, Munich

Picture credits:
Tom Roch

Additional photos:
Corbis: p. 29. Folio ID: p. 30.
GU: p. 26 (J. Rickers).
Jalag: p. 6 (Ch. Dahl).
Jump: p. 13, back cover inside (K. Vey).
Zefa: p. 19.
Rapoport, I. C.: p. 10.

Illustrations:
Heidemarie Vignati

For their support in photo production a special thanks goes to:
IKEA, Eching; C & A, Munich; Kokon, Munich; Reebok Germany, Oberhaching

Production:
bookwise Medienproduktion GmbH, Munich

Translation:
Lusia Ciurak

Important notice
The author and publisher have made every effort to ensure the information provided in this book conforms to national health and fitness standards and that the exercises are suitable for healthy individuals. It is not meant to replace the advice of a physician. Each reader is asked to make a personal decision as to which exercises are appropriate and how closely they want to follow the advice in this book. Neither the author nor publisher can assume responsibility for any injury, loss or harm resulting from the practices offered in this book.

ISBN (10)   0-7607-8495-7
ISBN (13) 978-0-7607-8495-2

Printed and bound in China

1 3 5 7 9 10 8 6 4 2

Foreword

When I first came across Pilates, I was fascinated by the precision with which the trainees did the exercises, moving in a kind of horizontal dance. Yet, at the same time, I also asked myself what was supposed to be so very different and new about this training method when the exercises really didn't seem any different to the exercises of other workouts.

When I began with my very own Pilates training program I quickly realized the big difference between Pilates and the many other body conditioning methods: With Pilates I was training not only my body, but I also had the opportunity to get to know myself better. I learned to observe my body more closely and to judge my physical capabilities better. I also noticed where I was physically and psychologically tensed up. Soon after, I was able to apply the knowledge gained in training to my daily life.

Would you like to do a workout that trains your entire body and gives you the chance to discover yourself at the same time? Use this book to train and get first-hand knowledge about what is so special and unique about Pilates. Do the body check, put together your very own personal training program and just plunge into the world of Pilates. You'll get a comprehensive theoretical and practical overview of the Pilates training method and you'll also find a wide selection of exercises, from basic to advanced, from Pre-Pilates to the original Pilates exercises. This is a book for everyone at every level of experience!

Antje Korte

A workout for
body and soul

Is the enormous popularity of the Pilates training program only the result of clever advertising? Not at all! Pilates is a gentle, effective, diverse and fun training program that everyone can easily learn. Follow in the footsteps of Hollywood stars and get acquainted with Pilates!

What is Pilates?

Pilates is a very gentle and effective workout that enables you to strengthen, shape, stretch and relax your body. In just a very short time, Pilates can help you improve your posture, correct poor posture and strengthen your physical and mental well-being.

The Pilates body conditioning program originally incorporated a series of calisthenic movements performed on padded mats, as well as additional repetitive exercises carried out on special equipment developed by Joseph Pilates himself. Precision and a gentle flow of movement, as well as the highest possible degree of tension release and natural deep-breathing, are typical of this workout and the basis for quick, tangible and visible results. The brain is activated through the total concentrated effort on the individual movements, channeling all thoughts into what is happening in the body and enabling an alert mind to do the exercise properly.

The Pilates program lets you tighten, tone and shape your body, as well as train your body awareness, rewarding you with a wonderful feeling of physical and mental well-being. Just experience for yourself how Pilates leaves your mind refreshed and alert and puts your soul in harmony. See how you can benefit from a more positive and unique vibrancy!

Muscle balance

Have you actually ever really thought about what the muscles in our body do while we are standing, sitting, walking or running? Well, in fact, quite a lot. Everything depends on the harmonious interaction and teamwork of the muscles. Muscles always work together with their counterparts and never alone. If a muscle contracts on one side, then its "partner" stretches on the other side, keeping the contraction within limits and within a healthy framework for the muscle. Very often this teamwork interplay becomes disturbed and unbalanced because we tend to use our bodies too asymmetrically: sitting too long in front of the computer, often carrying our children in the same position or carrying heavy shopping bags in the same hand. Illnesses and injuries also influence our body. An injured ankle or walking on crutches or with a cane often results in us assuming movements which safeguard the injured part of the body but bring the muscles out of balance. Over a longer period of time, these evasive movements cause certain muscles to contract in order to assume the same position. As a result, the counterpart muscles are permanently stretched, the contracted muscle is shortened, tight and cramped, and its counterpart muscle is stretched and weakened.

Mobilizer and stabilizer muscles

To understand the importance of muscle balance you have to know that there are two kinds of muscles that move our bodies. On the one hand, there are mobilizer muscles situated on the body's surface whose function is to move our extremities, i.e. our arms and legs. On the other hand, there are the stabilizer muscles located closer to the body's core whose function is to keep the torso stable while the mobilizer muscles move the extremities. Top-functioning stabilizer muscles make certain that the body maintains the best

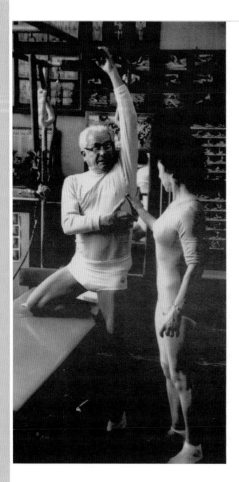

JOSEPH HUBERTUS PILATES

The Pilates method is named after Joseph Hubertus Pilates, who was born in Mönchengladbach, Germany in 1880 and died in New York in 1967. As a child Pilates was rather frail, weak and often ill. In his determination to strengthen his naturally weak constitution, Pilates occupied himself in his youth with many different types of sports e.g. gymnastics, fencing, skiing, boxing and wrestling, as well as tai-chi and yoga. Inspired by Eastern and Western training methods he developed his very own technique called contrology, a unique approach using precision and muscle control. While interned in England as a German POW during World War I, Joseph Pilates practiced and trained his methods with his fellow prisoners by attaching steel bed springs onto the walls. This was the first step toward the development of the special equipment that operates with steel bed springs even to this day.

He opened his studio in the New York City Ballet with his wife Clara, whom he met during his trip when immigrating to America in 1926. The close relationship between Pilates and dance intensified, and even famous dancers like George Balanchine and Martha Graham trained with Pilates.

Pilates continued training until he died at the age of 86 in New York.

possible position when moving and that the bones can move smoothly and easily in the joints.

The muscles weakened the most by this imbalance are the low-lying stabilizer muscles. If the stabilizer muscles are too weak, then the mobilizer muscles can no longer function optimally. They often try to stabilize the body themselves, and attempt to execute permanent movements they were not designed for. Soon the muscles are overworked, tight and cramped, the torso unstable and wear and tear on the joints develops as a result of poor posture. Headaches caused by neck tension, sciatica disorders and back problems are typical after-effects of an unbalanced interplay of muscle teamwork.

How does the Pilates training program work?

Pilates attempts to restore the natural muscle balance. During training, shortened muscles are stretched and their weakened counterpart muscles strengthened. First the overactive mobilizer muscles are disengaged during the basic training exercises, enabling the stabilizer muscles to operate alone and release the highest possible degree of tension to the adjacent muscles. For the simple Curl-ups (p. 58), it means you not only lift the torso, but also make certain that the thighs, buttocks, and neck are relaxed and refrain from "helping" the abdominal muscles; this way you can especially reach the low-lying abdominal muscles during the exercise.

In the course of the training program, special focused attention is paid to lengthening and strengthening the shortened as well as the overstretched muscles, because long muscles have more endurance, are less prone to injury and grant the joints the necessary freedom of movement. Long and strong muscles react like a marathon runner protecting the body during the day, whereas short, bulky muscles often seen in bodybuilders can ensure high per-formance for a short period of time, but can also tire very quickly and then become extremely prone to injuries.

What is the Pilates effect?

This is a constructive workout which tones and streamlines the body, especially female problem areas – e.g. abdomen, thighs and buttocks – improving and strengthening the body and reducing daily stress. A very attentive and observant workout prevents new muscle tension build-up, trains body awareness, strengthens coordination and improves posture.

A different approach – a different focus

For Joseph Pilates, his teaching method was a very personal and individual matter from both the teacher's point of view as well as the student's. He often developed special individual exercises for people, varying existing exercises and customizing them to their individual physical needs. This is probably the reason why Pilates never offered a training program to Pilates trainers, but worked closely together with different people who passed this method on after his death. The different approaches in which the Pilates method developed over the past decades were just as diverse as the people teaching them. There are some trainers who still teach the original Pilates exercises even today, i.e. physically challenging and almost acrobatic; others like to incorporate the original exercises with elements of yoga; and still others try to compliment the conditions found in fitness studios i.e. offering the training programs in bigger groups and at a very high sportive level.
The Pre-Pilates exercises were developed to meet increasing demands raised by rehabilitation and the desire and need to strengthen physical health, opening the doors to everyone. Pre-Pilates exercises help you to first strengthen the low-lying body muscles, carefully and gently preparing you step-by-step for the original exercises. In the introductory chapter there are a series of Pre-Pilates exercises that make starting easy.

Who is Pilates for?

Pilates is suitable for almost anyone who would like to do something good for his or her body. Dancers appreciate the Pilates training program in particular, because it offers more possibilities to stabilize and centralize. For example, dancers strengthen their potential by reaching and securing the power and energy necessary to perform dance movements from their body core (see also Pilates principles p. 15), and athletes, in general, like to use this fitness program as a supplement to their normal training .

And what about you? Do you have a very physically strenuous job? Then you can reduce muscle tension and discover relaxation with Pilates. The exercises balance out sit-down activities with just as much mental tension release. Pilates exercises are especially beneficial to your health offering post-natal conditioning, strength build-up at an advanced age and muscle build-up and physical strengthening after operations, injuries or illnesses. Who doesn't want to bring his or her body into the best possible shape and condition? Who doesn't want to get rid of tension or correct poor posture? If you are not sure if Pilates is the right method for you, then just simply talk to a Pilates trainer and express your wish to learn more about Pilates, and try it out! You'll enjoy it!

The Pilates method helps tackle unsightly fat deposits successfully.

The fundamentals of modern Pilates training

Have you ever spent hours sweating it out doing incredibly amazing exercises just to tone your abdomen and couldn't see any signs of success? It's aggravating. But this is what happens (and not only to you) if you are not aware of how to properly execute the movements. This is going to be different from now on with Pilates! During the exercises, concentrate on observing your body very carefully, noting how your body functions, where it is relaxed, where it is tense and which muscles are working during the exercise. By simply training muscles that need toning you'll experience a feeling of success and eliminate unwanted muscle tension. Another plus point is that you can also prevent unforeseen injuries and sprains because you will no longer be moving unawares, mechanically and overexerting your body.

The Pilates principles

The Pilates principles you are going to learn about in the following chapters form the basis for an effective training program. But don't worry! What may at first seem very theoretical will soon become second nature to you. All of the most important factors which have to be especially observed during the exercise will be repeated with every individual explanation. You'll quickly develop a routine checking individual points during training. The Pilates principles were set up by Joseph Pilates himself, taken over by different organizations, modified and expanded. In his book *Return to Life through Contrology*, Pilates himself names breath, control and concentration as the most important aspects of his training program. Today "Body control pilates", worldwide the largest Pilates organization, located in London, specifies the following eight principles as the most important for Pilates.

1. Tension release

Every exercise starts with tension release, because you can only reach the goal of your training program by releasing tension: a balanced, tension-free body. Observe yourself while peeling potatoes or working at your PC. Is it really necessary to raise your shoulders while working at the computer? Of course not. By being aware of tension release during the Pilates exercises you afford your body new posture and movement patterns and also enable your brain to sense and turn off tension in daily situations. The first step in training is tension release on a mental level. Don't set high standards for yourself, especially at the beginning! Be patient with yourself and give yourself time to experience Pilates!

Note: Tension release during the exercise doesn't mean total release. If you just lay there like "a sack of potatoes", body tension is obstructed and the muscles work ineffectively. "Relaxed" means to use just the right amount of tension for an exercise. If you do the "Knee Lift" exercise (p. 48), for example, you'll basically need to tense your muscles less than in the "Double leg stretch" (p. 96).

2. Center

Working from the body's central point is the be all and end all of Pilates training. Joseph Pilates called the body core the "powerhouse" – the area between the chest and pelvis to which the adjacent protective muscles belong and whose axis forms the spine. This area includes all of the important vital organs, attaches the arms and legs at the shoulders and hips and keeps you upright. Strong back and abdominal muscles protect your organs and back and take you through life free of pain. That is why all Pilates exercises aim at creating a strong body core.

The powerhouse muscles include:

> the low-lying diagonal abdominal muscles that stabilize the body like a corset and protect the organs. If you cough deeply, you can feel the muscles just above the pubic bone.

> the diagonal abdominal muscles that turn the torso to the side.

> the low-lying back muscles that are "stretched" between the vertical and horizontal processes of each vertebra and stabilize the spine working together with the diagonal abdominal muscles. Due to the conjunction of the abdominal and back muscles and in order to ensure a stable spine, the exercises training the abdominal muscles have to be done first.

> the pelvic muscles that complete the powerhouse from below and keep the organs in place. If the pelvic muscles are well-trained, they help to control urination and can provide you with a more enjoyable sex life.

Activating the powerhouse (p. 46–47) is the preparatory step described at the beginning of every exercise.

3. Breath

Breathing is the third important focal point of the Pilates training method. Since activating the powerhouse and breathing into the abdomen are impossible, Pilates developed a technique of breathing into the side of the chest (p. 44). Sounds complicated? Then try the following test. Tense up your abdomen using your muscles. Hold the tension, and now inhale deeply into the abdomen without releasing the tension. Doesn't work? It can't work. That is why breathing is steered through the chest, where breathing actually

THE MUSCULAR SYSTEM OF OUR BODY

Stabilizer muscles (below in blue) and **mobilizer muscles** (below in red) determine straight posture and keep our body flexible and agile. Using this diagram take a look behind the scenes and see which muscles the Pilates method specifically trains.

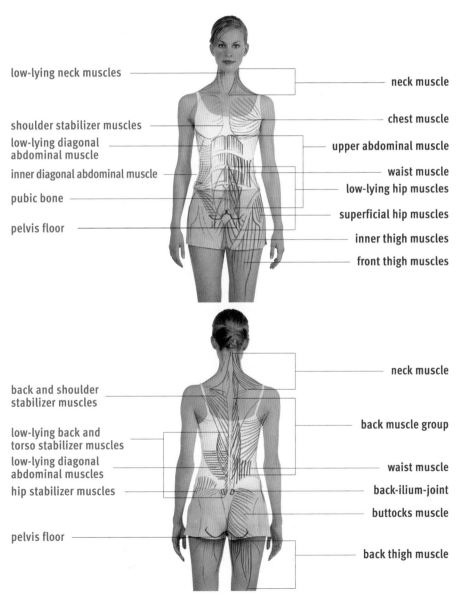

low-lying neck muscles — neck muscle

chest muscle

shoulder stabilizer muscles

low-lying diagonal abdominal muscle — upper abdominal muscle

inner diagonal abdominal muscle — waist muscle

low-lying hip muscles

pubic bone

superficial hip muscles

pelvis floor — inner thigh muscles

front thigh muscles

neck muscle

back and shoulder stabilizer muscles

back muscle group

low-lying back and torso stabilizer muscles

low-lying diagonal abdominal muscles — waist muscle

hip stabilizer muscles — back-ilium-joint

buttocks muscle

pelvis floor

back thigh muscle

takes place, namely in the diaphragm. Breathing into the side of the chest makes certain that the trainee can breathe easily during the exercise and still secure the tension of the powerhouse. A real Pilates specialty!

4. Positioning

Imagine a tower made of building blocks where one of the middle blocks is a bit out of sync. Shaky? Our body and the interplay of the stabilizer muscles behave just the same way. Where there's a part of the body out of order on a long-term basis is where the body is unstable, tight and cramped, overexerted and is prone to injuries. That is why the Pilates program attaches great importance to the correct positioning of the body during the exercise. Your body is optimally trained, and you learn to be aware of your poor posture on a daily basis and to change it, thus avoiding posture damage. Walking straight and tall with a tension and pain-free back gives you much more vigor and self-confidence than the most expensive pair of shoes or the most elegant wardrobe!

5. Concentration

It is concentration that fundamentally distinguishes Pilates from other training methods. For Joseph Pilates, concentration was the conscious performance of movement, as well as mind and body control during an exercise. What does this mean for you? Use all of your senses to concentrate on what is happening in your body. Correct your posture as soon as you notice a mistake or tense up.

Doing the exercises precisely is just one side of the coin. Your mind and thoughts are the other and they are just as important to the Pilates method. Don't get distracted! You'll definitely be successful in doing the exercises perfectly if you have your body and mind work together hand in hand.

6. Fluidity

If you watch children at play, you can see just how much endurance and how much fun they have running and jumping. Recent scientific studies have shown the importance of movement for learning and brain activity. Most adults could move more. The Pilates exercises are supposed to support the body during movement, since movement is the most natural thing in the world. Don't take long breaks and perform the exercises in a continuous, flowing movement, enabling the bones and muscles to work very efficiently, stimulating the flow of energy in your body and avoiding injuries caused by sudden, abrupt movements. When attempting the exercises, you may notice that each exercise has its own rhythm. The "Open leg rocker" (p. 100–101), for example, is a very peppy exercise, whereas "Stretching the neck" (p. 62) is a much slower exercise. But all of the exercises do have one thing in common: they are done gently and relaxed.
The gentler you do the exercises the more precise, more effective and more difficult they become!

> Our body needs to move – not only in childhood.

7. Integration

Pilates exercises call for the integration of a series of different elements: positioning yourself correctly first, tracking down tension (tension release) and then transfering and transporting your total attention through your entire body (concentration). You activate the powerhouse (breath, center) and perform the movements in question gently (fluidity), integrating all of these aspects and bringing them into harmony with one another.

The exercise "Hip Rolls" (p. 52), for example, requires that you go into the neutral position (p. 42–43) and take a moment to check your body for tension from head to toe and loosen up your shoulders, arms and legs. Then you inhale deeply, activate the powerhouse and move your knees to the side. Are your shoulders still loose during the exercise? Are the abdominal muscles still working together? Is your jaw all tensed up? Hold, and then return to the starting position.

Being able to integrate, the ability to keep an eye on details and apply them, improves with each training session and after some time doesn't require any mental effort anymore, as it will come instinctually.

8. Conditioning

In the Pilates program, conditioning refers to the endurance of the body's stabilizer muscles and not to cardiovascular endurance, somewhat comparable to high performance athletic training.

The objective of the Pilates training method is to strengthen the muscles so that you are in a position to work and function with an average degree of tension all day long and to move a strong and healthy body through the day.

Note: It isn't necessary to consciously initiate this kind of muscle tension. In a healthy, intact muscular system this happens automatically during the day! You'll notice if your muscles become more conditioned despite the increasing degree of difficulty because the exercises will seem to be getting easier and easier! For your daily routine, it means that jobs which used to be very strenuous suddenly aren't anymore or basically require less effort. For your body, it means that it is not only healthy, strong and agile, but that you have visibly streamlined and toned your thighs, abdominal and buttock muscles. A lovely side effect!

WHEN IS THE BEST TIME TO DO PILATES?

Is Pilates a training program that makes my body really fit all-around?

Absolutely! Pilates is a training program that totally mobilizes and strengthens the body. A balanced Pilates training program takes every single part of the body into consideration, balances it out, stretches and strengthens it, promoting muscle endurance, i.e. the ability of the muscles to take you healthy and upright through the day. But Pilates is not an endurance sport, i.e. it has no fortifying effect on the cardiovascular system. To get your body conditioning going you should supplement your training program with endurance sports like jogging, walking, swimming, cycling or inline-skating.

What do I have to look out for if I'm new at the Pilates training program? What's better at the beginning – personal training or matwork classes?

First and foremost, pay close attention to the quality of the training session. Choosing personal training or matwork classes is a question of personal taste. If you enjoy training with others, then join a matwork class, but if you prefer a very intensive and individual workout, then personal training is the right thing for you. A good basis for future training is to get to know your trainer and have him or her assess your body and its traits, features and qualities. So the rule of thumb for every beginner is: first treat yourself to a personal training session and test it!

Can I also do the Pilates training program if I am obese?

But of course! On the contrary, by exercising the low-lying muscles you can tone and tighten your body regardless of your body mass. Besides, strengthening the stabilizer muscles eases pressure on the joints caused by being overweight and can reduce pain caused by poor posture and being overweight.

Can I also do other sports in addition to the Pilates program or is it incompatible with other kinds of sports?

Pilates is anything but incompatible with other kinds of sports or gymnastics. On the contrary! Pilates enriches and compliments other workouts because it builds up the muscles optimally from the inside out, supporting your body awareness and training you to better observe your body. Gaining tangible and visible training results in other sports also comes more quickly.

Doing Pilates at home

Do you prefer trying out something new in your leisure time at home first? No problem. The tips on the next pages can help you put together your optimal at-home workout.

Just carefully read the tips on proper training first (p. 23), and then do your personal body check (pp. 32–36). By reading through the questions discussed on these pages and by making an exact observation of your body, you will quickly recognize which muscles are shortened and overactive and which could do with some strengthening. You'll get to know your body with all of its strengths and weaknesses. In the practice chapters starting on page 39, you will find a large selection of exercises for every level of difficulty that allow you to work on the Pilates training program independently, individually and comprehensively!

Give yourself time to master the book, be patient with yourself and simply enjoy these unique and wonderful exercises and the effects they have on your body!

The right way to train

When putting together your personal workout, it is important to consider not only the time factor. The degree of difficulty suitable to you, variety and allowing you to enhance your physical development as you go along are also all important. Trying it out is the name of the game! The different workouts presented in the exercise program at the end of the book (p. 116 onwards) help accomodate you when putting your exercise sequence together.

Points to bear in mind

Here are a few more tips before you start:

> **Follow the book exactly!**
All of the factors important for the Pilates training program are going to be presented page-by-page and one-by-one, and so you should study the exercises in the book step-by-step. In any case, start with the basic exercises to get a feeling for the fundamentals!

> **Don't try doing too much at the beginning!**
Try to concentrate on an exercise until you feel you have really understood it in both mind and body. At the beginning, work on one exercise a day until you have the basics down pat.

> **Follow the instructions about repetitions!**
You should really adhere to the number of repetitions indicated in an exercise. Don't try doing too much! If your body tells you it's enough, but your mind feels you should do another five repetitions, then just decide to trust your body.

> **Do the exercises slowly and conscientiously!**
Read the instructions carefully. From time to time, close your eyes during the exercises and probe your way inside to see how your body feels. Check for mistakes that have perhaps slipped in while doing the exercises.

> **Do the exercises with the least amount of effort!**
Do you have the feeling you haven't done enough? Well done! Do you tense up and find the exercises strenuous? Then you've done too much. Try the same exercise using a minimum of muscle strain. Better?

When shouldn't you train

> **Have a cold?** Sick people belong in bed and not on a mat. If you feel you are coming down with a cold, then it's better to look after yourself.

> **Eaten too much?** Give your stomach one or two hours to digest.

> **Backache?** Have your doctor or physiotherapist first clarify if the workout is advisable or not. Talking to your doctor is also advisable for anyone who is injured, has disk problems, or is undergoing other medical treatment.

> **Pregnant?** Even though Pilates is a very gentle workout, you should only train during pregnany if you already have previous Pilates experience and if you do the training program under the supervision of a professional Pilates trainer. You should also get the OK from your gynaecologist. Plus: Starting the abdominal exercises in the 13th week of pregnancy is taboo!

> **Had a drink or taken a pain killer?** If you've spent a lovely evening with friends and consumed alcohol or are under the influence of painkillers, don't perform the workout. Because both of these factors impair your natural sensitivity to pain.

TIP

ASK A PRO!

You've decided to train alone. Great! Nevertheless, you shouldn't hesitate to ask for advice if you have questions or if problems arise. Is there anything about the training program which puzzles you? Are you experiencing pain, or is there some other disturbing physical oddity which keeps cropping up during the exercises? Do you sometimes feel tense after the exercises? Or do you feel you're doing the exercises improperly? It doesn't matter. Wherever there's a problem, don't be afraid to ask a Pilates trainer for advice. It's best to make a special training appointment so that the expert can correct your problems quickly and quietly. You'll find addresses in the appendix and on the Internet.

How to handle pain?

Pain is not always bad, so it's a good idea to determine the difference. Feel and probe your way inside your body. What kind of pain are you experiencing?

> Only stretch as far as necessary without straining the muscles.

> **Is it stretching pain?**

Does it appear when you're holding the muscle in a stretch position? Then it is positive pain that occurs because the muscle is being gently pulled apart. The tension in the area adjacent to the shortened muscle is released and the muscle opposite can contract. Try to keep loose during stretching, and don't over-stretch your muscle.

> **Is it tension?**

Do your muscles feel hard and cramped? Are you possibly experiencing pain at a spot other than in the muscle being trained? Then you are doing too much of a good thing. Take it down a notch, and also pay close attention to the strained area during the exercise keeping it as loose as possible.

> **Is it muscle work?**

Yes, that's right. Even muscle work that you otherwise wouldn't notice can be painful. Make sure and see if the pain appears exactly in the spot being trained. Does it immediately disappear as soon as you've finished the exercise? Then this isn't real pain but a muscle working at top speed. If you train with less muscle tension, the "pain" gets better.

> **Is it a "hot" pain?**

Does it feel hot, as if it was running through your body like a fire? Or is it a stabbing pain, the kind you get with toothaches? If the pain doesn't stop even after you have completed the exercise, then stop! This kind of pain indicates an acute injury. Stop training immediately, and visit your doctor or other therapists to clarify the cause of the pain.

Turn off daily stress: Balance out, harmonize and let peaceful and relaxing music put you into the mood for your workout!

Preparing for the exercises

You'll enjoy your workout the most if you've taken the necessary preparatory measures. Take a few minutes and read the following points to get an easy start into your training program.

When's the best time?

There are no set rules as to when you should do the Pilates training. Get started when you feel the most energetic. Regardless of when you train, be sure to take your time and make sure the atmosphere around you is quiet and relaxed. Take the phone off the hook, put away your clock and turn on some lovely peaceful music. Do everything that helps you do your workout in a matter that is both easy and relaxed.

At the beginning, Joseph Pilates recommended ten minutes daily. Regular training was important to him because you develop the right feeling for the exercises and the body becomes supple and strong. These ten minutes a day, which you can, of course, increase, are ideal and recommended by Joseph Pilates himself. But it doesn't mean you can't do Pilates within another time framework. Think about just how much time you would like to and are able to invest in your training each week. Use the ten minutes, for example, as your daily chance to relax and prepare your body in the morning for the day ahead, or to leave the cares of the day behind you in the evening. Two or three times a week between 45 to 60 minutes are ideal for a complete training program. It doesn't make any sense to tackle this kind of a workout if you cannot fit it in anywhere into your daily routine. Then it is better to exercise ten minutes three times a week or half an hour twice a week rather than not at all for lack of time. You can do anything that makes you feel good, fits into your daily/weekly schedule, and don't give yourself a guilty consciousness if you perhaps haven't completed your set tasks. Be realistic about your resolutions!

Where's the ideal place?

If you set aside a room or space for your workout, you can totally concentrate on the exercises during the training session.

It is important to have the right room temperature so you can relax and so your muscles feel warm and pleasant. The first exercises in this book are not going to be very physically strenuous. Precision and concentration are required here. You won't sweat at the beginning, but it may be that your body temperature drops due to the tension release, and you start to feel a bit chilly. Turn the heat up a bit higher and enjoy the cosy warmth!

What should I wear?

Workout clothing should allow you unlimited freedom of movement and be tight enough so that you can look at your body in a mirror to check out particular areas. Choose comfortable and soft clothing in the "layered look" so you can take something off if it's too hot, or won't freeze during the gentler exercises. A top and a long-sleeved shirt on top go together with tight-fitting gymnastics leggings. If you freeze easily, put on a fleece vest to keep your muscles warm and supple. Complete your outfit by putting on warm socks, but you can do the Pilates workout barefoot just as well. Tennis shoes aren't necessary.

The necessary equipment

You really don't need any special expensive equipment to set up your own Pilates home studio. All you basically need are

> ❯ a blanket or mat
> ❯ a small and large towel
> ❯ a tennis ball and a flexband (or a scarf)
> ❯ a stool or chair with a hard but even surface
> ❯ a large mirror. It's good to have during some of the exercises, but isn't absolutely necessary.

How to put together your optimal training program

Every Pilates training program should be well-balanced and balanced out, meaning it should include strengthening as well as stretching elements. So be careful! In an at-home training program you tend to do the exercises that are easy and a lot of fun, and these are very often exercises that appeal to the dominant and overactive muscles anyway. So, get off easy street and overcome your baser instincts! Also try the positions and movements that are difficult when you have gotten a feeling for the exercises. Read the instructions carefully, try to do the exercise as properly and accurately as possible and consider them a challenge!

When training with this book, you should know that every single exercise block – beginners, intermediate, advanced – can be done separately. You should do the stretching exercises in the beginner's section according to your physical needs (see Body check, pp. 32–36), giving the strengthening exercises in blocks 2 and 3 priority.

Are you curious? Then get yourself something to write with and put together your personal training program using the tips in the next chapter.

PILATES IN A STUDIO

If you decide to take part in a Pilates course, you will come across very many different Pilates concepts. Take time to test the offers and "check out" your future trainer. This is important because the trainer can give you many helpful hints and tips and show you modifications that create the Pilates effect. You can only acquire this knowledge by taking a course and not at home, so it's more than imperative that you also like this person.

In general, the studio training program offers two possibilities:

> You can go to a matwork class.

    The matwork classes take place in small groups, and here you are taught the mat exercises that Joseph Pilates developed himself, as well as the modifications found in this book. Small equipment e.g. balls, flexbands or rolls are sometimes used during the floor exercises.

> You can train on the Pilates equipment.

    Training with equipment is done on the special equipment developed by Joseph Pilates himself. This apparatus has unusual names i.e. "trapez table", "reformer" or "chair", and functions by pulling or using a steel spring weight. This allows every Pilates student create his or her very own individual training program.
    On the one hand, by using the Pilates equipment you can consciously challenge your body and make an exercise more difficult. On the other hand, the equipment makes it possible to support the weak points of your body, e.g. using the Pilates equipment to have the body assume a position and do movements it otherwise wouldn't have been able to. Since working out on the Pilates equipment is part of the special personal training program, the decisive difference between both training forms is the more efficient and effective supervision and tailoring of the workout equipment to fit your specific individual needs.

Your personal training program

Are you looking for a workout that totally meets your needs? Then do the body check in this chapter and examine yourself in front of a mirror from head to toe – and please be objective! The answers help you put together a workout according to your personal needs. Relaxed or sweating, gentle or challenging – it really doesn't make a difference: Everything is possible with Pilates.

Do the body check!

There is an entire list of questions on the following pages. Please take some time to answer them so you can get an idea of the shape and condition your body is in, and where your strengths and weaknesses lie. To set up your own personal workout, you'll find recommendations for exercises at the end of every question. The best way is to just write the exercise into your individual training program under the individual categories (p. 37) – and your personal Pilates training program is ready to go!

Nevertheless, the "obligatory exercises" have already been entered into the training program because these Pilates basics are really very suitable to optimally prepare the body for each of the following exercises.

Of course, you can also incorporate exercises into your workout that bring you closer to your personal goal, be it your wish for more agility or more abdominal muscle strength or a more streamlined waist or, or ...

Take a quiet moment, look through the book and choose the exercises that especially appeal to you. If you are a newcomer to the Pilates training program, please start your training with the beginners exercises! If you have already had some previous experience with Pilates, you can venture out into the intermediate exercises.

Before you start training, you should get to know all of the other exercises that correspond to your level of performance. "Try them!" Get a feeling for the exercises! Which ones do you find especially effective, which ones are particularly pleasant and which are unusually difficult? Are you getting confused? Then gear down. First work on the easier exercises, and feel your way up, step-by-step to the more difficult exercises!

What type are you?

When putting together your workout, please make a note of question eight – your agility! Are you a very active person? Then complete your training program with stabilizing elements! If you are stronger, add more stretching and mobilization. By doing this, very active people acquire more muscle power, stabilizing their movements and safeguarding their joints, and strong muscular people become more agile and flexible, preventing their muscle power from stiffening their body.

Have you made a note of everything? Then let's get started! The complete training workout takes 45 minutes.

This is how it's done

To do the body check, you have to stand up straight in front of a mirror. Using the questions, take a good look at your body and check it from head to toe. Try to be objective about your body and don't look at it through "rose-colored glasses" by glancing down at your toned thighs or perhaps soft smooth arms. Stand normally during the body check. Everyone naturally tends to stand extra-tall, but you'll get better and more accurate results if you simply stand as you really are.

1. Head

? Does your head sit between your shoulders or more "in front of" your shoulders?
> In front of the shoulders: You need to stretch your chest and neck (p. 49, 66) and strengthen the shoulder stabilizer muscles (p. 50–51, 60–61, 62).
? Do you hold your head straight or is it slightly tilted to one side?
> Tilted to one side: Do the neck stretching (p. 66) twice to the side you tilt your head towards.

2. The neck and shoulders

? Can you trace a gentle horizontal line across your shoulders and collar bones, or does the line sweep upwards?

> Sweeps up: You need to stretch your neck (p. 66) and strengthen the shoulder stabilizer muscles (p. 50, 60–61, 62).

? When you look at yourself in the mirror from the side, are your shoulders situated along the side of your torso or are they hunched forward?

> Hunched shoulders: Stretch your chest muscles (p. 49) and strengthen your shoulder stabilizer muscles (p. 50, 60–61, 62).

3. The spine

? Look at your upper spine from the side i.e. the area between the spine and just below the shoulder blades: Is your upper spine flat or more arched back?

> Flat upper spine: In addition to stretching the back of your chest (p. 51), it would do you good to strengthen your ribs and abdomen (p. 58–59).

> Arched upper spine: You need to stretch the front chest muscles (p. 49) and strengthen the shoulder stabilizer muscles (p. 50, 60–62).

? Is your lumbar spine – the part of your spine between the ribs and hips – flat or hollow?

> Flat spine: Stretching the back of your thighs (p. 54–55) and strengthening the back (p. 76–78) and hip muscles (p. 48, 106–107) keeps the spine supple and agile and strengthens it in the right places.

> Hollow spine and strong adjacent muscles: You can mobilize and stabilize your spine by stretching your hip muscles (p. 56) and strengthening your abdomen (p. 46–47, 58–59).

? Please do the "Rolling down the wall" or "The wheel" exercise (p. 67). What does your spine feel like during the rolling movements? Does it roll down smoothly like a wheel or do you have the feeling that several vertebrae are moving together?

> Hedging and obstructive rolling means that one or more vertebrae are holding the muscle cords together due to over-

TIP

FLAT OR HOLLOW LUMBAR SPINE?

To determine the form of your spine, place the palms of your hands to the right and left of your spine. This is where you'll find your back muscles. If you can hardly feel these muscles, then your spine is more flat. If the muscles are so strong that they form a cavity in between, then your spine is more hollow.

IS THERE AN IDEAL SPINE?

Every spine has curves: The cervix and the lower spine bend forward (lordosis), whereas the upper spine and sacrum bend back (kyphosis). Some people have flatter curves, others are more defined, and every spine digresses more or less to the side (scoliosis). This only becomes a problem if the spine loses its mobility or stability, imbalancing and improperly straining the body. Therefore, it is important to maintain the mobility of the spine and to stabilize it.

activity and are preventing movement: Stretching the hip (p. 56) and back muscles (p. 57) brings relief.

4. The back

? Do you have backaches?
If this is muscular pain e.g. a tense neck, then the following exercises can help you. If the bones and joints have shifted and are causing pain (arthrosis, slipped disk etc.), then these exercises can help ease and relieve the pain.
> Backache in the neck and cervix: Stretch the chest and neck (p. 49, 50, 51, 66) as well as strengthen the shoulder stabilizer muscles (p. 60–62).
> Stretching (p. 49–50) and mobilizing (p. 51, 58, 62 or 78, then p. 99) helps with problems of the upper spine.

> You should try to stretch your back or hip muscles (p. 56, 57, 66), stabilize your back further by strengthening the powerhouse (pp. 46–48, 58) and mobilize the spine (p. 52–53) if you have pain along your spine.

5. The abdomen

? Is your abdomen soft and round or more flat and tight? Are your neck and cervix tense during the abdominal exercises?
> If you feel tension in the neck and cervix during the abdominals exercises, and/or if you have a soft round abdomen, then your low-lying abdominal muscles are a bit weak. You need to do some gentle strengthening (p. 46–47, 58, 59, 71).

6. The hips

? If you look at yourself from the side in the mirror, are your hips an extension of your spine, or do you push them slightly forward?
> Pushed forward: Stretch the back of the thighs (p. 54–55) and strengthen the abdominal (p. 46–47, 58, 59) and hip muscles (p. 48, 106–107).

? Do you have sciatica pain?
> If you do, stretching and strengthening the buttocks brings relief (p. 64, 65).

7. Legs, knees and feet

? When you stand up straight with your feet together, your knees together and stretched and you bend over, can you touch the floor with your hands?

> No floor contact: Stretch the back of the thighs (p. 54–55).

? How do you brace your legs?
> If your knees are overstretched to the back, you also need to stretch the back of the thighs (p. 54–55) and strengthen the hip muscles (p. 48, 74, 106–107).

? Do your knees point forward or face each other?
> Face each other: Stretch the hip muscles, buttocks and the inner thighs (p. 56, 57, 65) and strengthen the buttocks (p. 65, 76–77, 79).

8. Agility

? If you go down on all fours and point your fingers straight ahead, where do the hollows of your arms point to?
> If the hollows of your arms point forward, then you are probably a more flexible and agile type of person, and should integrate more stabilizing exercises into your training program. Make sure to maintain a good position during the stretch exercises.
> If the hollows of your arms face each other, then you are probably a more strong and muscular type of person. Integrate a lot of stretching exercises and exercises to mobilize your spine into your program.

MY PERSONAL TRAINING PROGRAM

If you make a copy (or two) of this plan and fill it out, you can always put together new training programs and have them at your fingertips as you flip through the book. Using the body check, fill in the empty blanks with the exercises suitable for you. If you are a beginner, start with the beginner's chapter, even if more difficult exercises were specified in the body check. You don't have to fill in all of the blanks and it isn't necessary to do all of the exercises indicated in a block during every training.

Your balanced-out Pilates training program should include the following elements:

Warm-up – Basis stabilization

Activating the powerhouse .... p. 46–47

Stretching exercises for the back, muscles, hip muscles, back of the thighs, inner thighs, buttocks

Stretching the back of the thighs ... p. 54–55

....

....

....

Strengthening the hip stabilizer muscles and low-lying hip muscles

Knee lift .... p. 48

....

....

Stretching the neck, shoulders and chest

Neck stretch .... p. 66

Arms open .... p. 49

Shoulder drop .... p. 51

Strengthening the shoulder muscles

Arm control .... p. 50–51

Shoulder stabilization .... p. 60–61

....

....

Strengthening the powerhouse

Curl-ups .... p. 58

Side curl-ups .... p. 59

....

....

Strengthening the low-lying back stabilizer muscles and back muscles

Stretching the neck .... p. 62

....

....

The bundle .... p. 77

Mobilizing the spine

Spine roll-up .... p. 52–53

Hip rolls .... p. 52

....

....

Cool-down

Rolling down the wall/The wheel ...... p. 67

Chalk circles .... p. 69

The
workout

Have you taken all of the necessary preparatory training measures? Well then, just plunge into the pleasure of Pilates! Get started with the exercises on the following pages: Shape and train your body, stretch it, strengthen it, and tone it. Get to know its potentials, its limits, its needs, its likes and dislikes, and discover what it can look like when it's in top shape!

Beginners: Mobile and stable from the very beginning

This chapter is going to acquaint you with Pilates exercises that might seem very easy and simple at first, but are very important for muscle balance. By the way, when you are doing the exercises you will quickly realize that these exercises are not as easy as they seem.

Even if you have already had some previous experience with the Pilates training program, you should do these exercises, especially the Pilates basics (pp. 42–47), to strengthen the low-lying muscles of your body. Doing a few beginner exercises as a warm-up is an ideal way to prepare yourself for the more difficult exercises in the chapters ahead. Moreover, the gentle lengthening and stretching help you find out where there are overworked and shortened muscles in your body.

Pre-Pilates exercises: Gentle groundwork

The exercises in this chapter are exclusively pre-Pilates exercises. They were actually developed to prepare the body in the gentlest possible way for the somewhat complex and very physically demanding original exercises. The positive side effect of these exercises is that the body is stabilized inside and out and relieved of tension and pain caused by poor posture. How does this work? A picture can say a thousand words.

Our body: A tree

Imagine a big old tree with wide-spreading branches and thick foliage. If this tree didn't have strong firm roots, then the gentlest breeze could blow it over. Our body functions the same way. The low-lying muscles of our power-house stabilize the body and make sure that the muscles closer to the surface do not obstruct body movement. The stabilizer muscles could be considered the roots of our body and their optimal, strong and firm condition is imperative for you as a healthy human being. The pre-Pilates exercises are extremely suitable for stimulating and strengthening the stabilizer muscles because the least amount of movement can keep the more superficial muscles disengaged. Returning to our example of the tree: If the tree has a strong and firm foothold in the ground, then the branches can sway gracefully in the wind.

This is the true challenge of the pre-Pilates exercises: It's not difficult to raise a knee (p. 48), but it can be very difficult indeed to raise the knee using the

powerhouse with a scooped belly, an activated pelvis and stable hips that remain absolutely firm and fixed during lifting.

Since our "body tree" also needs a lot of flexibility in addition to strong roots to be able to rock in the wind, the pre-Pilates exercises are supplemented with a series of stretching exercises that optimize both your body's agility and mobility.

Pilates basics: Basis stabilization

The Pilates basics on this and the following pages are exercises that have a very gentle effect and acquaint you with a few very important facts about Pilates training: the neutral position, breathing into the chest from the side, activating the pelvis and the powerhouse. As a preparatory measure, these Pilates basics will be specified before every individual exercise.

Neutral position

The neutral position of the pelvis is the basis of Pilates training and the starting position for numerous Pilates exercises. The neutral position releases tension in the spine and strengthens its natural curves.

> Lie on your back. Place a folded towel under your head. Spread your legs a hips' width apart bending your knees at a ninety-degree angle. Rest your arms long by your sides.
> Practice the following different positions at a comfortable pace:
> Roll your hips into the mat beneath you until your spine sinks flat into the mat and your hips lift slightly. **1**
> Then lean and tip your hips until a hollow forms in your spine. **2**
> Now place your hands at the height of your waist beneath the spine and let your back sink gently into your hands,

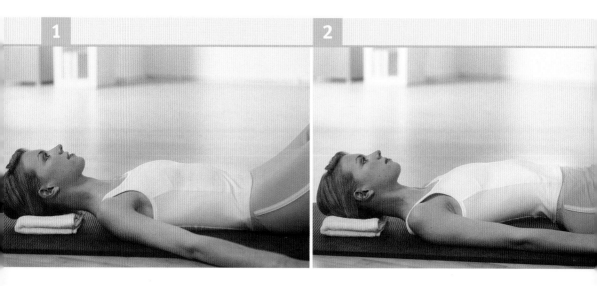

just as if you had wanted to warm your hands. Don't press.

> Then again place your arms next to your body. This is the correct neutral position. **3**

> Take a few relaxed deep breaths in the neutral position.

> To get rid of tension in the legs, shake your knees a few times. Your feet and shoulders sink into the mat.

Note: If you feel tension in the shoulders or spine, roll your head slowly and gently from side to side. Try to do the movement with less physical tension!

> **Modification:** When you have mastered the neutral position, you can do it together with the exercises "Knee lift" or "Small knee circles" (p. 48)

RELAX!

This is an ideal position for relaxation. Try it out after a hard and stressful day's work! Simply lie down, feel the mat beneath you, lift up your body weight, and breathe deep and easy.

TIP

3   Repeat 2 or 3 times in every position

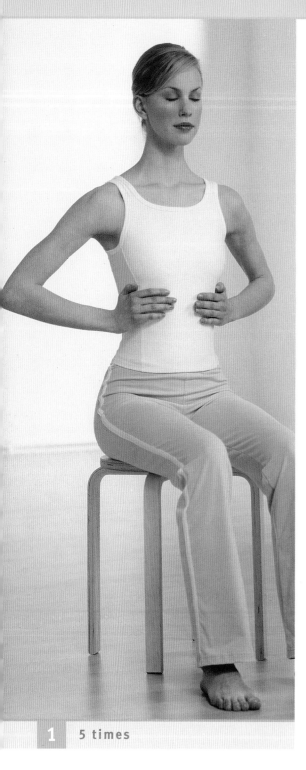

Breathing into the chest

"Breathing into the chest" is a very vital part of the Pilates exercises. It mobilizes the muscles between the ribs, helps you to breathe deeply and intensively and stabilizes the powerhouse from above. During the challenging original exercises, breathing into the chest supports and cooperates with the powerhouse, maintaining its tension. The instructions "inhale deeply" and "inhale in preparation", described on the following pages refer to this kind of breathing.

> Sit up straight on a stool with a hard surface, and spread your legs a hips' width apart.
> Place your hands on the side of your rib cage.
> Press the rib cage lightly with your hands, and as you inhale, try to push the ribs apart with your hands. **1**

Note: Is your belly very arched? Do your shoulders and breastbone lift? None of this should happen. Concentrate on breathing only into the area below your hands. A mirror can be helpful here.

1 | 5 times

Activating the pelvis

The pelvis and the low-lying abdominal muscles form a muscular unit, substantially cooperating to stabilize the torso. The instructions "lift hips" and/or "squeeze the buttocks together" refer to this kind of hip/pelvis workout, aiming at strengthening the pelvic muscles.

> Sit up straight on a stool.
> Roll up a towel, and sit on it stride-saddle. Spread your legs a hips' width apart placing the back of your hands on your thighs, your neck is long.
> Inhale deeply. As you exhale, lift up your hips gently putting more pressure on the towel.
> Hold your hips. Try to squeeze your buttocks together gently without engaging your bottom.
> Continue breathing normally, count to five in your head, and then slowly release.

Note: Do not let your shoulders and jaw work together, especially here, and there should be no visible changes taking place either. The hips do not roll. Make sure you do not create a "tube feeling" below i.e. no feeling at all, as if you were sucking something in. Imagine your hips are a hammock you are lifting.

2   5 times

Modification: Hip elevator
> Imagine your pelvis floor is an elevator with three storeys, and try to strengthen and release the tension step-by-step.

Activating the powerhouse

"Activating the powerhouse" incorporates the individual components of the first three exercises and provides the preparatory measures for all of the exercises to follow. Before you attempt doing any of the exercises on the following pages, bring your torso into the most neutral position possible for your hips, spine and shoulders first. Inhale, and as you exhale, activate your powerhouse. When you have mastered activating your powerhouse, you do not have to do the first three exercises of this block separately any longer, but you can connect them with one another instead.

This exercise is a rather unspectacular exercise requiring only a bit of effort,

but it is nevertheless one of the most important preparatory exercises for the most difficult exercises. Work with a minimum of tension! The instructions "activate your powerhouse", "lift up your hips and the navel sinks toward the spine", "as you exhale, stabilize" refer to this exercise.

> Go into the neutral position. Place your hands on your ribs.
> Inhale deeply.
> As you exhale, gently lift up your hips, and let the abdominal wall sink toward your spine. **1**
> Keep your belly scooped for a count, continue breathing normally, and release the tension again.

Note: Make sure your hips remain fixed and firm. Placing your hands on your groin or under your waist can help you avoid cheating. In these positions, you should not feel any movement in the hips whatsoever. Your shoulders should be absolutely easy and relaxed.

Modification: Shinbone press

For the more difficult versions of these and other exercises you will really need a stable powerhouse. The following exercise helps you get a feeling for it:

> Go into the neutral position. Grab your shinbones cradling them with your hands just below the knee. You may lift your head. **2**

> Breathe normally and press your shinbones gently against your hands. Let your abdominal wall fall and your spine sink into the mat beneath you.

> Imagine your back is soft, and let it fuse with the mat. You should not feel any unpleasant pressure in your spine.

> Release your hands, and try to hold the position for a few counts. **3**

> Relax between repetitions.

2

3   3–4 times

1 Each side 3 times, always alternating

Stable hips, stable shoulders

Knee lift

Simple, but oho! The "Knee lift" is especially effective in stabilizing the hips and torso and strengthening the abdominal muscles.

> Go into the neutral position placing your hands on the mat.
> Inhale.
> As you exhale, activate your hips, and let your navel sink gently toward your spine.
> Put your entire body weight consciously onto the mat, and then slowly lift up your right knee a few inches keeping your hips fixed and firm. **1**
> Inhale again with lifted knee, and as you exhale, renew the tension of the powerhouse, and lower your leg.

Note: Keep your hips as firm and stable as possible. Observe yourself carefully: Is there tension in another part of your body? Are your shoulders relaxed? Is your neck long?

Modification: Small knee circles

> Lift your knee as in the original exercise above, and place a flexband close to the hollow of your knees behind your thighs.
> Relax your thighs, activate your hips and abdominals, and try to draw small circles on the ceiling with your knee without moving your hips.
> Repeat on each side three times.

Arms open

The "Arms open" exercise combines
two very important exercises with one
another. On the one hand, it wrings out
your spine like a wet towel, something
you'll really enjoy, and on the other hand,
it strengthens the hips and stretches the
decollete.

> Lie on your side. Place two towels
  rolled together under your head,
  stretch your arms out long in front of
  you. Bend your legs forming a ninety-
  degree angle with your hip and knee
  joints. Rest your knees on top of one
  another. **2**

> As you exhale, stabilize, reach out
  with the top hand, lift your arm
  opening it to the ceiling, and let it
  float behind you.

> Follow your hand with your eyes, your
  spines rolls, the shoulders are wide and
  open and the knees together. **3**

> Reach until you feel stretching in the
  shoulders, hold this position for three
  relaxed counts, and return to the
  starting position.

Note: Make sure your knees remain
together, and keep your shoulders down
and away from your ears!

THE WINDSHIELD WIPER

TIP

In the end position, gently move
your arms up and down toward
your head and feet, and watch
to see if the stretching becomes
more intense.

1 5 times

Arm control

The "Arm control" is one of the most important exercises used to stabilize your shoulders and relieve neck tension. The instructions "integrate your shoulders", "keep your shoulders down and away from your ears", "the shoulders are wide and open" refer to the kind of shoulder workout where the shoulders are consciously gently pulled down.

> Go into the neutral position.
> Inhale deeply, and as you exhale, activate your powerhouse.
> Let your hands glide along the mat toward your feet. Then raise your arms and hands toward the ceiling, and move them in a semi-circle behind your head. Your arms are outstretched, becoming an extension of your body, your shoulders are pressed down tightly i.e. far way from your ears. **1**
> Press until you feel stretching in the nape of the neck or your upper arms, stabilize again, and return to the starting position.

Note: Before lifting your arms, push them toward your feet! Keep your arms long even if you have proceeded

TIP

HIPS + SHOULDERS = ONE

Imagine that your shoulder blades are connected to your hips with a thick rubber band that moves downward as you raise your arms.

to move them behind your head. Are your shoulders pressed away from your ears? To test this, just lift your shoulders up high once, and return to the starting position. As soon as you notice that your shoulders pull up, drop your arms!

Shoulder drop

This is a wonderful exercise to do for tense shoulders or after a stressful and strenuous day. It helps to stretch and relax the neck as well as the muscles between the shoulder blades and promotes the mobility of the upper spine.

> Go into the neutral position, and stretch your arms out long to the ceiling.
> Inhale and exhale relaxed. As you inhale, raise your left arm up to the ceiling so that the arm is outstretched and pointing slightly diagonally to the right, your shoulders lift, and your head and chest roll gently to the right. 2
> As you exhale, let your shoulders glide back gently into the starting position. Keep your arm outstretched to the ceiling.

Note: Make sure your shoulders glide back gently as if into a soft feather pillow and not onto a hard concrete floor. This is supposed to be a relaxing exercise!

2 Each side 3 or 4 times

A supple spine

Hip Rolls

One of the best exercises used to mobilize the spine! Another plus point: It stretches the back muscles.

> Go into the neutral position keeping your feet and knees together. Stretch your arms out to the side.
> At first inhale, and, while you exhale, activate your powerhouse by gently pulling in your hips and abdominal muscles.
> Move both legs to the left and roll your hips in one direction and your head in the opposite direction. Roll your hips only as far as your shoulders can still maintain a relaxed position on the mat.
> If you notice that your opposite shoulder wants to lift off the mat,

stabilize again and gently roll your hips back.

Note: It is quite possible that you roll too far to one side or the other during this exercise. Thus simply concentrate on the rolling movement and on your shoulders!

Spine Roll-up

This exercise stretches the back muscles and makes the spine supple. It is especially important for people with a severe lordosis i.e. with a severe hollow back near the waist and lower spine.

> Go into the neutral position. Place a tennis ball between your knees.
> Inhale deeply and relaxed.

> As you exhale, lift up your hips and let your navel sink toward your spine. Squeeze your buttocks together until your spine gently rolls into the mat, and the hips lift up slightly. **2**

> Inhale again, and as you exhale, activate your powerhouse, release your shoulders, and roll back into the neutral position.

> With each new roll, roll a few inches higher **3** until you have completely lifted up your spine. **4**

Note: Imagine your spine is a pearl necklace. Really try to roll up each individual vertebra. Roll only to the midback, or only as far as the lower tips of the shoulder blades, keeping contact with the mat. Any movement beyond that point strains the neck and cervix! You shouldn't feel any pressure in the spine, but if you do so, make sure you do not roll too high!

Your shoulders are very tempted to help you roll down. Try to sink relaxed into the mat beneath you.

4   5 times

Stretching: Mobilizing the hips

Stretching the back of the thighs

"Stretching the back of the thighs" is a relevant part of the most important exercises used to mobilize the hips as well as the hip and knee joints. People with a sit-down job or people who tend to push their hips forward when standing will benefit the most from this exercise. The first part of the exercise applies to the top fibers of the muscles, whereas the modification exercise refers to the lower muscle fibers. Always do the exercises together.

> Go into the neutral position. Place a small rolled towel under your spine, and place the sole of your left foot flat on the mat bending your left leg. Prop up your elbows, and relax your shoulders. Place the flexband around the sole of your right foot, keep your leg lifted, and grip the band with both hands.

> Inhale, and as you exhale, lift up your hips and let your navel sink toward your spine.

1   Repeat each side once

> Pull your right knee up toward you without increasing pressure onto the towel, and stretch your thighs to the ceiling until you feel the stretching start. Keep your leg bent! **1**

> Continue breathing normally, count backwards slowly from 15, and then release the position. Continue with the modification.

Note: Pay close attention to your shoulders keeping them as loose as possible. Let your tailbone sink into the mat beneath you.

Modification: Lengthening the out-stretched leg

> Now place the sole of your left foot onto the mat bending your right leg, and stretch the right leg with the flexband to half level. **2**

> Stabilize again, and move the out-stretched leg toward the ceiling without rolling your hips into the towel. **3**

> Relax, count backwards from 15, release, and change sides.

> In the end, you can lengthen the calf muscles by pushing out your heels. Ugh, that hurts!

Note: Keep your shoulders loose and continue breathing normally.

2

3 Repeat each side once

Stretching the hip muscles

If the hip muscles are shortened, they tend to tip the hips forward, negatively influencing your entire body alignment and causing slipped disks and other nasty problems. Lengthening, therefore, is very important.

The following stretching exercises lengthen these muscles and mobilize the knees, hip joints, hips and spine.

> Go into the neutral position. Place your buttocks on a big rolled towel, pull your knees up to your chest and place your thighs on your abdomen.
> Take hold of your left leg with both hands in the hollow of your knee.
> As you exhale, activate your hips and abdominals, and place your right leg, as it is, without changing the angle of the knee, as close as possible to the

rolled towel on the mat. Do you feel pulling in the top part of the thigh of the right leg? Good! **1**

> Hold this position for five deep and gentle counts, and try to let your thigh muscles become a bit softer with every breath.
> Now extend your right leg so that you feel pulling in the right groin, and count slowly backwards from 20. **2**

Note: In the second part of the stretching exercise do not let your spine lift off the mat. Your leg doesn't have to touch the mat, because it is more important to have an outstretched leg.

1

2   Repeat each side once

Stretching the back muscles

Shortened back muscles, that press the spine together stripping it of its "elbow-room", are a typical cause of backache. This exercise lengthens the back muscles and mobilizes the spine.

> Go into the neutral position. Place your hips on a large rolled towel and your arms out long by your sides.
> Pull your legs up toward you one by one. To strengthen and intensify the stretching, you can clasp your legs with your arms. Let your spine fuse with the mat. 3
> Inhale into your entire torso, and feel how soft your spine becomes.
> Rest a moment.

Stretching the inner-thighs

Stretching the muscles on the inner side of the thighs is especially important for people who have a weak pelvis or who suffer from sciatica.

> Go into the neutral position. Rest your hips on a large rolled towel.
> Stretch your legs up.
> Open your legs, and let them fall gently to the sides. 4
> Rest for five short counts, and then bring your legs together again.

3 Repeat once

4 2 times

1 Repeat 5 times, then change hands

Strengthening the abdominals

Curl-ups

Curling up the torso is simply the exercise for strong abdominal muscles and a strong and healthy back! Work with minimum effort so that you can really reach the stabilizer muscles.

This exercise strengthens the low-lying abdominal and back muscles, the muscles between the ribs and the shoulder stabilizer muscles. It tones and tightens the hips and mobilizes the upper spine.

> Go into the neutral position. Rest one hand on your abdomen and place your other hand under your head.

> As you exhale, activate the powerhouse. Then bring your chin toward your chest, lift your head, and focus your eyes on your knees. **1**

> Curl up only as far as you can, keep your belly scooped and not hunched. Hold this position for a count, and then release.

> Your shoulders are wide and open i.e. your body is loose and uncramped, your belly is scooped, and your hips neutral.

Note: Make sure to keep your neck long. Do not press your chin to your chest, but rather let it "hover" above your chest. Your hips should remain stable. Watch your groin: Do you feel any tension there? Then place a large towel under your knees and stretch out your legs.

Do not lift up your shoulders at all!

2 Repeat each side 5 times

Side Curl-ups

Curling up to the side strengthens the diagonal abdominal muscles and enhances a slim waist! The same rule also applies here: Use minimum effort.

> Go into the neutral position. Place both hands behind your head and your feet side by side. Squeeze a tennis ball between your knees.

> As you exhale, stabilize, and move both knees six inches to the left.

> Stabilize again, then lift up your elbows slightly, bring your chin toward your chest, lift your head, focus your eyes on your knees. **2**

> Keep your shoulders integrated and wide apart, have your chin "hover" above your chest, and scoop your belly.

> Hold for a count, and then release.

Note: Make sure your knees do not pull your torso to the side. Keep your body weight centered and your hips firm and stable. Your shoulders are wide and open.

RELAXING YOUR ABDOMINALS

After completing the abdominal exercise, treat yourself and your abdominal muscles to a quiet relaxing moment: Extend your arms and legs and stretch yourself out to a full body's length!

TIP

Repeat circling 5 to 10 times

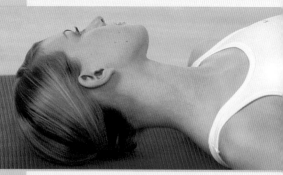

Strengthening neck, shoulders and back

Nose circles

"Nose circles" is an exercise that appeals to the low-lying neck muscles. After completing the abdominals exercise, it quickly and efficiently eliminates neck tension.

> Lie on your back, stretch your legs out.
> Relax and breathe. To release neck tension, roll your head once to the right and then to the left.
> If you like, close your eyes, and start drawing circles as big as quarters in the air until your neck feels supple and relaxed. **1** – **4**
> Reverse directions half way through.

Forward flexband pull

These two exercises require very precise movements. Here only use minimum effort. It's a very good idea to sit in front of a mirror to watch and check yourself. Pulling the flexband strengthens your shoulders, straightens up your back and supports the powerhouse. Before doing this shoulder stabilizing exercise, you should treat your front and back chest muscles to some stretching, depending on what you need ("Arms Open" p. 49, or "Shoulder Drop", p. 51).

> Sit up straight on a stool. Spread your legs a hips' width apart.

5 | 5 times

6 | 5 times

> Place the flexband around the back of your hips, hold it loosely with both hands so that your hands rest on your thighs, and the band is loose.
> Inhale deeply, and let your shoulders "float" gently to your ears.
> As you exhale, activate your power-house.
> Integrate your shoulders by pushing your hands down gently, and with your arms outstretched, move the band forward as far as possible keeping your shoulders pressed down. **5**

Backward flexband pull

> Sit up straight on a stool. Spread your legs a hips' width apart forming a ninety-degree angle with your thighs and hips.
> Place the flexband around your knees, and hold on to it loosely to the side at about the middle of the thighs.
> Inhale deeply, and pull your shoulders slightly up to your ears.
> As you exhale, push your hands down and out, and with arms outstretched pull back gently. **6**

Note: Work using your powerhouse, and do not swing.

Stretching your neck

"Stretching your Neck" is one of the most important exercises used to strengthen the back and shoulder stabilizer muscles. Practise this exercise regularly before doing the other back exercises and always apply only the least amount of effort! Enjoy a relaxed neck.

> Lie on your stomach. Place your hands on top of one another, and rest your forehead on your hands.
> Inhale deeply. As you exhale, activate your powerhouse.
> Let your shoulders move and float back. By doing this, your neck stretches and your head lifts a few inches off your hands.
> Focus your eyes on your hands, your neck is long and your shoulders relaxed. Keep your buttocks loose, and your elbows free of pressure.
> Hold your breath, and then release.

Note: Be careful of your buttocks and do not let them help your back muscles during this exercise! Also pay close attention to your elbows. You lie on them, but do not apply any pressure.

1   **6 or 7 times**

The arrow

This is a super way to strengthen your entire body, especially the back muscles.

> Lie on your stomach. Rest your arms long by your sides. You can place a towel under your forehead to protect your nose from any unnecessary pressure.
> Inhale deeply, and as you exhale, stabilize.
> Then lift your shoulders up off the mat and move them gliding toward your feet.
> Lift your arms, point the palms of your hands to your thighs. Your neck is long and your head lifts. Keep your buttocks and legs relaxed. 2
> Hold for a count, and then relax.
> Stabilize again, and repeat the exercise by pushing out your legs with feet outstretched. Push until they slightly lift, engage your buttocks, and stretch out from head to toe! 3

Note: Really lift your shoulder blades off the mat. Try to do the first modification of the exercise with relaxed buttocks challenging your back all the more!

2   3 times   3   3 times

1 5 times

EASING MENSTRUAL PAIN

If you suffer from menstrual pain, then "Pillow Press" is an excellent exercise you can use to help relieve tension and cramps in the lower abdominal muscles.

Stable hips

Pillow Press

The "Pillow Press" is one the most effective exercises for people with weak hip or abdominal muscles, stimulating the hip and low-lying torso stabilizer muscles as well as the muscles of the inner thighs. In addition, it relaxes the back-ilium-joint and the groin going down really deep! Here too: Use minimum effort.

> Go into the neutral position, and rest your hands on your groin. Place a folded towel under your head and a rolled towel between your knees.

> Inhale. As you exhale, lift up your hips, let your navel sink toward your spine, and press the rolled towel together gently. Keep your hip muscles supple and your shoulders totally loose and relaxed. **1**

> Count slowly backwards from five, and then release.

Note: Do not do too much! Keep your hips fixed, firm and stable, disengage your buttocks and relieve your hands of any tension drawn from the hip muscles (the top of the thighs). Oh, by the way: Is your neck relaxed?

| 2 | 10 times | | 3 | Each side 2 times |

The oyster

"The oyster" is a wonderful "bottom booster" and often eases sciatica pain! Always do both of the exercises on this page together.

> Lie on your side. Extend your lower arm, and place a small towel between your head and arm. Bend your knees, and align your feet with your spine. Prop up your top arm in front of you, and integrate your shoulders. Lift up your waist slightly i.e. you can push your top hand flat between the mat and your waist to check.
> Inhale. As you exhale, activate your powerhouse, and open your top knee toward the ceiling. 2
> Keep your torso stable, hold this position for a count, and then release again.

Buttock Muscle Stretch

This stretching exercise relieves sciatica pain or knock-knees. It mobilizes the back-ilium-joint and the hip joints.

> Sit up straight on a stool, and spread your legs a hips' width apart. Place your lower left calf on top of your right knee.
> As you exhale, stabilize, and with a straight upper body, lean forward until you feel stretching in the buttocks. 3
> Count slowly backwards from 15, release the tension, and repeat the exercise.

65

1   Repeat each side twice   **2**   Repeat each side once

Stretching the buttocks-waist-neck

The waistline stretch

This exercise tones and tightens the waist and eases back pain.

> Sit up straight on a stool. Spread your legs apart forming a ninety-degree angle with your knee joints.
> With a straight torso, lean to the left and prop your left elbow on your left knee. 🔢
> With an active powerhouse lift your right arm and move it slightly diagonally toward the ceiling.
> Hold this position stable, continue breathing normally, count backwards from ten, and release your position.
> Intensify the stretching very gently the second time around.

The neck stretch

This is a wonderful exercise for people who often suffer from neck tension!

> Sit up straight on a stool. Let your arms hang down loose to both sides.
> Focus ahead, and let your head sink toward your left shoulder.
> Activate your powerhouse, and let your right hand "float" to the floor. 🔢
> Count slowly backwards from 15, and release the position again.

Note: A tense neck has already gone through a lot of suffering anyway, so stretch very gently.

Cool-down

Rolling down the wall: The wheel

The "Rolling down the wall" exercise or "The wheel" helps you get a feeling for the agility and mobility of your spine. Pay close attention as to how your spine rolls each vertebra down off the wall.

> Stand up straight with your neck pressed flat against a wall, place your feet eight to ten inches from the base of the wall, bend your knees slightly, and keep your hips neutral (push a hand between the back of your waist and the wall to check). Relax your shoulders against the wall making sure your head has no contact with the wall. Hang your arms down loosely to both sides.

> Inhale deeply.

> As you exhale, activate your pelvis, and sink your navel gently and deeply toward your spine.

> Then bring your chin to your chest and roll each vertebra down off the wall until your hands touch the floor.

> Inhale, and as you exhale, activate your powerhouse again, and roll back up until your shoulders and not your head touch the wall.

Note: If you still cannot keep your belly scooped, stop this movement and breathe.

4   4 times

Intermediate – A big step forward

The training program presented in the beginner's chapter has prepared you for the exercises ahead. Hopefully, you have been able to relax and use the power of your mind during the exercises by concentrating on your movements and have also got a first-hand feeling of how your body should behave during the exercises. You have already raised your sense of body awareness.

In this chapter you will be confronted with exercises that are based on the beginner's exercises. Your objective will be to connect these exercises with one another and to intensify them. In the introductory chapter, for example, you have specifically learned to tense your hips by breathing into your chest from the side and to activate your powerhouse. In the following chapters you will combine these three exercises more and more into a complete unit. Your strong powerhouse then provides the basis for challenging abdominal exercises, protecting you during the back exercises and enabling you to specifically strengthen the hips and perform the rolling movements for the spine. There are also several exercises that prepare you for the original Pilates exercises.

For further training, it is important not to rush ahead. You should give yourself and your body a few weeks time to get a feeling for the following exercises. After awhile, you will notice you are aware of things in your body you couldn't feel at the beginning of the training program.

Warm-up

Chalk circles

This is a wonderful exercise used to relax your spine and a great start into the training program. It stabilizes the hips and mobilizes the spine, as well as stretches the front chest muscles.

> Lie on your side. Place two rolled towels under your head. Straighten your arms out in front of you (cf. "Arms open", p. 49). Bend your legs forming a ninety-degree angle with your hips and knees. **1**
> Activate your powerhouse.
> Slide your top hand forward along your lower hand letting your top hand draw a big circle on the floor around you. Maintain contact with the floor as long as possible. **2**
> Breathe normally while drawing the circles.

Note: Keep your knees together and your arms outstretched!

1

2   Repeat each side twice

The roll-down

"The roll-down" is a rewarding challenge for people with a severe hollow back! This is a very beneficial exercise because it mobilizes the spine, effectively stretches the back muscles and also strengthens the abdominal muscles.

> Sit up straight with your knees bent. Place a hand under each thigh, your elbows are wide and the shoulders are integrated.

> Inhale, and as you exhale, stabilize.

> Initiate the roll-down from your tailbone to your spine, or to the point where you have the feeling to be able to still keep your balance. Pull up your feet by sliding them along the mat toward you. **1**

> Pull your navel back into your spine again, release your hands from under your thighs, and roll down an inch. **2**

> Then roll back up to the starting position chest first, keeping your back arched.

Note: Keep your spine arched during the entire exercise. Roll up with your chest first and not your head! Press your shoulders to your chest and not toward your ears!

1

2 4 times

3　4 sets

More power to the abdominals

The hundred I

"The hundred" is one of the most characteristic and unusual Pilates exercises. The special feature of this exercise is the pumping motion of the arms. By inhaling and exhaling for several counts, "The Hundred" enhances muscle tone and conditions the stabilizer muscles.

> Go into the neutral position. Rest your arms by your side.
> As you exhale, activate your power-house.
> Lift your chin to your chest, raise your head, stretch your arms long by your sides reaching toward your feet, and then lift your hands off the floor. **3**
> Hold your powerhouse, continue breathing normally and pump your arms straight up and down as if you were slapping water.
> Inhale for five counts, exhale for five counts.

Modification: The hundred II

> Activate your powerhouse. Without moving your hips, lift up, bending your knees one by one, keeping the lower thighs in a horizontal position.
> Do the exercise and the pumping motion as mentioned in version I. Let your chest and belly sink into the mat beneath you.

Note: Keep your back flat and belly scooped throughout!

Pump with your upper arms, stretch your arms long by your sides, and keep your shoulders pressed away from your ears.

Single leg stretch I

The original "Single leg stretch" presents a great challenge to your coordination. That is why we are going to proceed slowly. This exercise strengthens the powerhouse, especially the diagonal abdominals, and tones your body core and thighs.

> Go into the neutral position. Lift your legs bending your knees at a ninety-degree angle. Place your hands on your knees. 1

> As you exhale, activate your powerhouse, lift your head tucking your chin into your chest.

> Sink your spine gently into the mat, and stretch out your right leg diagonally resting both hands on your left knee. 2

> As you inhale again, bend your right leg.

> Stabilize again as you exhale, and stretch your extended leg out long. Your belly remains scooped, the shoulders are wide and the neck long. Focus your eyes on your belly button.

> Securing the muscles of your powerhouse, pull back your leg, inhale, and stretch your right leg, extending it diagonally out and long as you exhale.

Note: Make sure to keep your shoulders stable! Let your torso sink into the mat beneath you keeping it as still and stable as possible. Keep your belly scooped. Breathe deeply!

1

2 Repeat each side 4 times

3

4   **Repeat 4 times**

Double leg stretch I

The "Double leg stretch" requires total control of the powerhouse. This exercise works and strengthens the powerhouse and shoulder stabilizer muscles and tones the abdominals and legs.

> Go into the neutral position. Rest your arms long by your sides, lift your legs bending your knees at a ninety-degree angle. 3

> As you exhale, activate your powerhouse, lift your head tucking your chin into your chest.

> Reach forward with your hands, and stretch out your arms in the air, parallel to the mat, extending your legs to the ceiling.

> Sink your spine into the mat, focus your eyes on your belly button. Pull your navel back into your spine. 4

> Hold two or three seconds, and then release again.

Note: Integrate your shoulder blades by pulling your arms way down. Make sure your chest is wide and open. Secure the muscles of your powerhouse, and watch as your navel sinks deep into your spine.

1 **Repeat each side 3 times**

Teaser: Preparation

This "hard nut" is a typical Pilates exercise that can be quite demanding and shows just how acrobatic Pilates originally was.

This exercise strengthens the shoulders and hips as well as the powerhouse, focusing especially on the diagonal abdominal muscles, and tones the legs, arms and body core.

> Go into the neutral position. Place the soles of your feet flat on the mat. Rest your arms long by your sides.

> Inhale deeply, and as you exhale, activate your hips and abdominals.

> Then lift your head tucking your chin into your chest and stretching your arms out long. Arch your spine, and roll your spine down gently into the mat.

> Reach out with your arms parallel to the mat, and lift your left leg diagonally. Focus on your left knee, pull your navel into your spine, and hold for several counts. 1

Note: Make sure your shoulders are wide and away from your ears. Keep your hips still, and secure the stable neutral position.

A balancing act

Open-leg rocker: Preparation

The "Open-Leg Rocker" is not suitable for people with severe neck problems, and since it is also difficult for people with shortened back thigh muscles, it is better to stretch first! (p. 54–55)
This exercise strengthens your body deep from within and works on your physical balance.

> Sit up straight with the soles of your feet flat on the mat and your knees bent. Take hold of your ankles on the outside.

> Activate your powerhouse, then let your navel sink down deep until your spine arches, your body weight shifts to the back, and your feet lift.

> Stabilize again, integrate your shoulder blades, and stretch out your neck.

> Straighten your right leg gently and accurately to the ceiling.

> Hold your leg for a few counts, and then straighten out the left leg.

> Hold for two or three seconds, and release again.

Note: Keep your belly scooped! Let your shoulders rest on your chest! If you rock too much, take hold of your legs a bit closer to your knees!

3   2 times

A strong and agile back

The star I

"The star" invigorates your body awareness, enhances coordination and stabilizes your shoulders.
> Lie on your stomach. Stretch out your
  arms and legs.
> As you inhale, stretch out your hands
  and lift them up.
> As you exhale, stabilize, pull back your
  shoulders letting them glide toward
  your feet.
> Press down lightly on both hands,
  stretch your neck and lift your head.
> Shift your body weight onto the left
  hand, and lift up your right arm four
  inches. **1**
> Hold one or two seconds, and release
  again.
Note: Keep your legs and buttocks
relaxed. Make sure to keep your shoulders down as far as possible. Focus your
eyes on the floor in front of you.

Modification: The star II
> Place your hands on top of one
  another and your forehead on your
  hands.
> Activate your powerhouse as you
  exhale, and thereby integrate your
  shoulders.
> Press your right foot lightly, stretching
  your leg, and lift the left leg a few
  inches off the mat. **2**
> Hold for a few counts, and then
  release. Keep your hips stable on
  the floor.
Note: Make sure to press your shoulders
away from your ears! Your hips are
tempted to lift up with the raised leg,
so keep them firmly on the floor.

2 Each side 3 times   **3** Each side 3 times

Modification: The star III

> Lie on your stomach and stretch out your arms. Reach out with your hands as you inhale.

> As you exhale, activate your power-house. Pull back your shoulders keeping your elbows extended.

> Place your weight onto your left hand and right foot, and lift up your right hand, left leg and head. **3**

Note: Make sure the position of your hips and shoulders correspond to the above-mentioned instructions, and only do this modification if you have really mastered the first two versions!

THE BUNDLE

You should always finish back exercises by arching your back! Go into a crouched position, and let your torso rest on your thighs for a few moments. Then roll yourself up "peeling" off each vertebra. If the position seems too difficult, do the back muscle stretch exercise (p. 57).

TIP

1

2 3 times

Small arches

The "Small arches" mobilize the spine and strengthen the back muscles and shoulder stabilizers. You should be careful with this exercise if you have back problems. Do the exercise very carefully, and lift up only a few inches. The "Small arches" is a challenge for people with a strongly arched back!

> Lie on your stomach. Place your forehead on a towel, your hands directly next to your shoulders and your elbows close to your chest.

> As you exhale, activate your powerhouse. **1**

> Let your shoulder blades glide along your back toward your feet. Lift up your head stretching out your neck.

> Gently press down your hands and elbows, and "peel" your head and torso off the mat, sinking your elbows into the mat.

> Keep your belly scooped, and stretch out your neck. Hold for one or two seconds. **2**

Note: Be careful of pain in the lower back! Lie down again, and first lift up only a few inches; try lifting up a few inches more perhaps next time.

DO THE BUNDLE OVER AND OVER AGAIN!

Definitely wind up this exercise with the Bundle (p. 77)! And watch yourself very closely as you do the exercise: Are you experiencing aches and pains or is there something else bothering you? Well, it shouldn't. You ought to stop doing the exercise immediately.

IMPORTANT

Heel beats

The "Heel beats" strengthen the back, the entire buttock muscles and the back of the thighs. Careful! Breathing fluctuates here. Beat your heels while exhaling in a pumping motion, just as if you were blowing up a balloon.

> Lie on your stomach. Stretch out your legs and spread them a hips' width apart slightly turning out your feet and knees. Place your hands on top of one another, rest your forehead on your hands, and integrate your shoulders.

> As you exhale, activate your power-house.

> Integrate your shoulders again, then press your feet lightly into the mat so that your knees lift. Keep your legs straight holding both legs a few inches in the air. 3

> Stabilize again, and as you exhale, beat your heels together, just as if you were holding a balloon between your legs.

Note: Finish off the exercise with the "Bundle" (p. 77), engaging the hip stabilizers by stretching the buttock muscles.

3 **Complete 3 sets of 10 beats**

The cat

This exercise strengthens the torso stabilizer muscles and enhances straight posture. Stretch and bend like a cat, and arch and lengthen your spine!

> Get down on all fours. Spread your legs a hips' width apart, place your hands directly under the shoulders, point your fingertips. Place the inner side of your elbows facing each other. (If not, bring and keep your arms in this position to avoid incorrect strain and overstretching of the elbow joints during the exercise).

> Press the heels of your hands lightly into the mat thus stretching your arm and lifting your spine. Your neck and spine are long and as agile and stable as a steel spring.

> As you exhale, stabilize by gently squeezing your buttocks together. Your navel sinks into your spine.

> Then roll your spine up arching the lower back and chest, focus your eyes on your knees. Keep your shoulders wide and open.

> Inhale again, and release the position: Your tailbone pulls back and out, your neck lengthens and glides up, your belly is scooped. Your shoulders are wide and open.

Note: If your wrists hurt, shift your weight more to the back!

1

2 5 times

3   Repeat each side 3 times, always alternating

The eye of the needle

This exercise twists your spine as if you were wrangling out a towel. The spine just loves this movement and, basically, can use it several times every day. The deep-lying back stabilizer muscles as well as the broad back muscles also enjoy this stretching movement.

> Get down on all fours. Spread your legs a hips' width apart, place your hands directly under your shoulders. Most of your body weight rests on your knees.
> Inhale.
> As you exhale, stabilize. Place your weight onto the left arm, lift the right arm, and let the back of your right hand glide along the mat through the space between your left knee and hand.
> Push your hips a bit to the right, and bend your left arm. Your right shoulder approaches the mat, and your neck is outstretched. **3**
> Hold for three or four seconds, and return.

Note: Keep your shoulders wide and open. Make sure your neck is outstretched and the hips stable. Do not let your arm pull you over.

| 1 | 5–10 times | 2 | 5 times |

Slender arms, toned legs, a "tight tummy"

The drinking lion

"The drinking lion" is a gentle modification of push-ups. This exercise strengthens the front and back arm and abdominal muscles, and unlike push-ups is suitable for everyone.

> Get down on all fours. Lengthen and stretch your spine, integrate your shoulder blades making sure to keep them wide apart. Place your hands on the mat facing each other, and point your fingertips.

> Activate your powerhouse, and lengthen your spine, bending your elbows out. Keep your neck long and the shoulders wide and open. 1

> Press down gently onto the heels of your hands stretching your arms again.

Modification: "The drinking Lion" for the back muscles of the upper arm.

> Point your fingertips straight out and your elbows back.

> Activate your powerhouse, lengthen your spine, and bend your elbows toward your feet. 2

> Do not turn your elbows out, keep your shoulders integrated and neck long.

> Bend only as far as you can hold the position comfortably, and shift your body weight to the back.

Note: Pay close attention to your shoulders. Do not shrug and drop your shoulders. Since the hips are tempted to push back, it is important to hold the position firmly!

Leg-pull down: Preparation

The "Leg-pull down" is an excellent exercise that strengthens and tones your entire body. This exercise requires an extremely stable powerhouse.

> Get down on all fours. Lengthen your spine, place your hands palm-down onto the mat underneath your shoulders, place your legs a hips' width apart, point your fingertips forward.
> Press the heels of your hands into the mat stretching your neck and arms, and lifting your spine, aligning it with your chest and neck. Focus your eyes on the space between your fingertips.
> As you exhale, activate your power-house, press down your left foot lightly, and push it back along the mat until it lifts, and you can lift up onto your toes and the balls of your feet. [3]
> Secure the muscles of your power-house, and extend your second leg going into a push-up position. [4]
> Then, with an activated powerhouse, first pull back the left and then the right knee toward you.
> Now start with the other leg.
> Keep your spine long and your power-house active.

Note: Keep your neck and head long, and focus your eyes on the space between your fingertips. There is a tendency to let your head hang down and to let your spine sink in between your shoulders.

3

4   Repeat each side 6 times

Strong shoulders, stable hips

Shoulder bridge: Preparation

The "Shoulder bridge" incorporates mobilizing the spine and strengthening the back of the thighs and buttocks. A real "bottom booster"!

> Go into the neutral position. Place your hands on your groin.

> As you exhale, activate your powerhouse, gently squeeze your buttocks together, pull your navel deep into your spine, roll your spine into the mat, lift your hips, and roll each vertebra up to the center of your chest. ▮1▮

> Stabilize again, shift your body weight onto your left foot, and lift the right foot about four inches off the mat.

Keep both hips level and stable, and relax your shoulders. ▮2▮

> Put your foot down directly and gently, lift up the hips again, if necessary, and raise your left foot.

> Put your foot down, lift up in the hips, and roll down the vertebrae of the spine like the pearls of a necklace.

Note: Do not hold your breath! Breathe normally, and make sure your shoulders are relaxed.

1

2   Repeat each side 3 times

3 | Repeat each side 4 times | 4

Torpedo

Turn your body into a torpedo, and stretch it out in two different directions. This is an excellent exercise used to tone your legs and body core!

> Lie on your side. Stretch your lower arm up and out, straighten out your legs tilting them slightly forward. Place a folded towel between your head and arm. Align your upper arm with your lower ribs, and press your shoulders away from your ears.
> As you exhale, stabilize and raise the top leg four to six inches.
> Activate your powerhouse again, and lift up the lower extended leg. 3
> Count back slowly from five, and relax.

Note: Do you feel the muscles working more in the lower back rather than in the waist or abdominals? If you move your legs a bit more forward, and your hips move back, you can feel your abdominal muscles.

Modification: Balance!
> Try to lift your upper arm, and keep your balance. 4

A WALL SUPPORT

If you lie directly against a wall, you can control your optimal position best. Align your shoulders and hips, and stretch your legs slightly forward. Careful: Do not lean on the wall! Use the wall only for orientation.

If you have strong, broad buttocks, support your upper back with a sofa cushion.

TIP

Cool-down

Rolling like a ball

"Rolling like a ball" is an exercise which incorporates all of the Pilates principles relating to body tension. It massages the spine and is a lot of fun!
This exercise is more demanding than you would think and should always be done on soft padding. Best of all is on the training mat.

> Sit up straight placing the soles of your feet flat onto the mat. Place a hand under each thigh.

> Shift your body weight backward, and pull up your legs toward you, lifting your feet off the mat, and arching your spine. Keep your elbows extended wide, and integrate your shoulders.
> Inhale deeply, and as you exhale, stabilize.
> Reinforce the arch in your spine by raising your knees closer to your body. Focus your eyes on your belly button. Keep your shoulders wide and open. **1**

1

2   5 time

> With your back arched, roll to your shoulder blades, keeping your head and neck up. **2**
> Let your chest roll, flowing forward.
> Keep your balance. Do not put your feet down!

Note: Always keep your back arched. If you have difficulty rolling back, then you are swinging too much with your legs. Let your nose lean forward instead.

Do not roll back too far, because this strains the neck. Roll only to your shoulder blades! And always use a mat!

Modification: Small and compact!

> If you grab your shins with your hands, you are working your abdominal muscles even more! **3**

Advanced: Pilates for gurus

Welcome to the original Pilates! The following chapter exclusively contains exercises developed by Joseph Pilates himself. If you have reached this point, you will have already experienced the real Pilates and optimally prepared and strengthened your body for the original exercises.

Now you are getting down to serious business. After completing the preparatory beginner and intermediate level exercises, you are now well-prepared to give your body the finishing touches. But take your time! The following rules also apply to advanced learners: Don't rush through the exercises and don't forget to do the "easy" exercises! Integrate the exercises you know and have been doing for several weeks to carefully and completely strengthen your muscles over a longer period of time. If you omit this step, then you are neglecting the deep stabilizer muscles, and you are weakening your muscle balance. Just take some advice from Joseph Pilates who often said: "Rome wasn't built in a day" meaning – be patient with yourself!

Warm-up

The hundred III

This version of "The hundred" requires a very strong powerhouse. It stabilizes the torso and shoulders and strengthens the abdominals, arms and thighs.

> Go into the neutral position. Rest your arms by your sides. Raise your legs, and bend your knees at a ninety-degree angle.
> Inhale deeply.
> Then activate your powerhouse, lift your chin to your chest, lift your head, stretch your arms long by your sides, and reach forward until you feel the bottom of your shoulder blades gently pressing into the mat beneath you. Stretch your legs to a forty-five-degree angle. **1**
> Focus your eyes on your belly button.
> Pump your upper arms straight up and down.

Note: If you perform most of the movements with your shoulder blades, or you cannot keep your legs stretched out, return to the intermediate version of "The hundred" exercise (p. 71).

1 5 times when inhaling, 5 times when exhaling | at most 20 sets

Roll-up and down

The "Roll-up and down" is a good exercise used to "lubricate" the joints between the vertebrae, strengthening the abdominals and the shoulders at the same time and stretching the back. Looking back and forth at pictures one, two and three, you will notice a flowing sequence of movements.

> Lie on your back. Stretch out to your body's full length bringing your straight arms forward over your head. **1**

> As you exhale, activate your powerhouse.

> As you inhale and secure the muscles of your powerhouse, pass your arms over your chest.

> Then bring your chin to your chest, lift up your head, and as you exhale, roll up each vertebra. **2**

> Focus your eyes on your knees, and point your toes. Push your arms parallel to the floor, arching your back, and reaching forward to your feet. **3**

> Keep your navel pulled back into your spine, and roll yourself back by squeezing your buttocks together. The bottom of your shoulder blades rolls back gently, and each vertebra slowly uncurls back down into the mat.

> Maintain a scooped belly, and integrate your shoulders.

Note: Keep your shoulders pressed away from your ears. Do not try arching your back by pushing your head forward, but consciously pull back your heels instead when rolling down, pressing them gently into the mat.

Modification: Palms up

> It is beneficial to turn your palms up, stabilizing your shoulders when rolling down with outstretched arms.

> If you still have difficulty rolling up, pull yourself up by anchoring your hands underneath your thighs.

This is great trick to do when rolling down:
Sit up with your heels off the mat. As you exhale, stabilize, and initiate the rolling movement by pulling your heels up toward you, as if your feet would want to return to the mat or disappear into your pant legs. This way your spine arches almost automatically!

3 3 times

The rollover

"The rollover" is a wonderful exercise used to mobilize and massage the spine. This exercise requires a lot of physical tension and strong abdominal muscles since it strengthens the abdominals, back and arms, stretches the back of the thighs, buttocks and the back muscles, and tones all of the areas involved. Leave out this exercise if you have a bad neck. Photos 1–2–3–2–1 present a sequence of movements.

> Go into the neutral position. Close your legs and straighten them to the ceiling. Extend your arms long by your sides. 1

> Inhale, and then activate your power-house as you exhale.

> Press the palms of your hands gently into the mat, lift your legs off the mat and up and over your head.

> Lift from the back of your hips controlling the movement with your power-house muscles, and using your arms, roll your spine down feeling each vertebra.

> Roll to the middle of your chest. Your legs are outstretched, just a bit above a horizontal position. 2

> Keep your powerhouse firm, stretch out your heels, and spread your legs a hips' width apart. 3

> Press your wrists firmly into the mat sliding them forward as you go.

> Now slowly roll back again into the starting position.

Note: Be careful about the position of your head, neck and shoulders. Remember to keep your head on the mat. If you have difficulty keeping your head on the mat, then do the easier versions of the exercise, i.e. "The drinking lion" (p. 82) and "The leg pull-down" (p. 83), and train the back of your upper arms. Keep your neck stretched as long as possible.

3 3 times

Rolling down can be easier if you maintain a good hand position, i.e. arms long by your sides, your wrists sinking into the mat beneath you and your fingertips stretched out. Keep your belly scooped!

Modification: Knees bent and a "soft" ball

> This exercise is easier if you slightly bend your knees starting from the point where you feel you can no longer hold the positon when rolling down.

> Placing a rolled towel or a soft, half-inflated ball under your lower back safeguards your last few vertebrae until your abdominal muscles become stronger!

Single leg circles

The "Single leg circles" stabilize the hips and torso and strengthen the buttocks and abdominals. Doing the "Small Knee Circles" (p. 48), prepares you for this exercise.

> Lie on your back with your legs extended and your arms long by your sides.
> Inhale. As you exhale, lift your hips pressing your navel deep into your spine.
> Gently straighten the left leg to the ceiling at a ninety-degree angle.
> Keep your powerhouse firm and active. Keeping the hips as still as possible, draw small circles on the ceiling with the extended leg. Keep your right leg long and outstretched. Then exhale consciously when moving your leg across your body.
> The bigger the circles the more you challenge your powerhouse.
> Draw five cirles in each direction, and then change legs.

Note: Keep your arms absolutely relaxed and sink them into the mat without applying pressure. Make sure to keep your hips firm and stable at all times.

Modification: Bent knee

> If you find it very difficult to stretch your leg vertically, you can either pull your other leg up from the mat or slightly bend your outstretched leg, and pull your knee up toward you.

1 5 times in each direction **2**

3

4 **Each leg 4 or 5 times**

Strengthening the powerhouse

Single leg stretch II

The more difficult version of the "Single leg stretch" tones and strengthens the powerhouse and legs, and challenges your coordination.

> Go into the neutral position. Lift your legs, bending your knees at a ninety-degree angle, and place your hands on your knees.

> As you exhale, activate your power-house. Your torso lifts up, and your spine sinks into the mat beneath you. 3

> Take hold of your left leg alongside your ankle with your left hand, grasp your knee with the inside of your right hand, and pull your knee to your chest with both hands, extending your opposite leg in front of you. 4

> Keep your navel pulled into your spine at all times, integrate your shoulders, keep your torso stable.

> As you inhale, pull back your right leg, and then hold both knees for a moment.

> As you exhale, switch legs, keeping your head and shoulders pressing down. The movements are slow and precise.

Note: Your body should tense up into the extended leg. Imagine you are reaching for a light switch with your toes.

1

2 4 times

Double leg stretch II

The second version of the "Double leg stretch" is a very high hurdle for the abdominal muscles to clear. Follow the instructions very carefully.

> Go into the neutral position. Lift your legs off the mat, and bend your knees at a ninety-degree angle, placing your arms long by your sides.

> Activate your powerhouse as you exhale. Inhale deeply, and lift your head onto your chest. Reach your arms out long, and raise them a few inches off the mat. Extend your legs straight to the ceiling. **1**

> Keep your upper back arched and belly scooped, focus your eyes on your belly button, and as you exhale, stretch your arms above your head. **2**

> Hold a second or two, pull your arms back, and release.

Note: Do not let your head fall back as you stretch your arms above your head. Press your shoulders down and away from your ears, and leave enough space for your neck.

3

4   **Repeat each side 4 or 5 times**

Single straight leg stretch

The "Single straight leg stretch" strengthens the powerhouse, especially the abdominals, and tones the legs.

> Go into the neutral position. Lift up your legs, bend your knees placing your hands on the side of your knees.

> Inhale, and as you exhale, activate your powerhouse.

> Lift your head to your chest. Press your spine deeper into the mat, and extend your legs straight up to the ceiling. **3**

> Secure the muscles of your power-house, grab hold of your left ankle with both hands as you stretch your left leg long in front of you while lowering the opposite leg. Pull your navel into your spine, the shoulders are pressed down and the elbows extended out, and focus your eyes on your belly button. **4**

> Inhale, and raise both legs. As you exhale, stabilize again, and then switch legs.

Note: Keep your torso perfectly still. Imagine it is firmly anchored to the mat.

A supple spine, a "tight tummy"

Crisscross

The "Crisscross" works your entire body and mobilizes the spine, duly challenging the abdominals and waistline.

> Go into the neutral position. Lift up your legs, bend your knees, and place your hands behind your head.

> Inhale, and as you exhale, activate your hips and abdominals.

> Lift your head, bring your chin to your chest pressing your spine deep into the mat. **1**

> Twist the upper part of your body until your left elbow touches your right knee, extend your left leg long and above the mat in front of you. **2**

> Inhale, bring your leg back, keep your shoulders straight so that your eyes focus on your belly button.

> As you exhale, stabilize again, and change sides. Keep your torso anchored to the mat and as perfectly still as possible. Press your shoulders down and away from your ears, and scoop your belly.

Note: Keep your shoulders integrated i.e. far away from your ears. Keep your elbows as extended as possible, and do not allow them to fold in, but rather twist around the entire shoulder area. During this exercise it is especially important to anchor your body core to the mat, because the steadier you remain, the more effectively you are working your abdominals.

1

2 Each side 3 times alternating

3

4

The saw

The name "The saw" expresses the feather-like movement with which this exercise is done, stabilizing the hips and mobilizing the spine. It works the back of the thighs, the waistline and all of the back muscles.

> Sit up tall with your legs extended, spreading them apart slightly more than a hips' width. Push your heels out from under you. Press your heels and buttocks down into the mat beneath you. Stretch your arms out to your sides at shoulder level so that you can still see your hands from the corners of your eyes.

> Activate your powerhouse, then twist from your waist to the left and touch your outer left shin with your right hand stretching your left arm back and up.

Keep your eyes focused on your left hand. 3

> Inhale deeply, and in three small steps, push your right hand along your shin to your ankle exhaling deeply every two to three inches. 4

> Keep your legs extended, your knees pointing up and your body weight anchored in both buttocks.

> Inhale deeply, hold, and then exhale.

Note: Keep your shoulders pressed down and away from your ears. If you feel tension in your neck, place your left hand directly next to your hips with the fingertips pointing out. Keep your eyes focused on your left hand.

Open leg rocker

The "Open leg rocker" works you from head to toe, strengthening body balance and stabilizer muscles, and enhancing your posture. As a reminder, take a look at the preparation exercise on p. 75. The photos 1–2–3–2–1 show a sequence of movements.

> Sit up tall. Place your hands alongside your shins and as close as possible to your ankles, keep your elbows straight, integrate your shoulders, and extend your spine toward the ceiling.
> Inhale at first, and activate your powerhouse.
> Shift your weight slightly back by pulling your knees toward your chest and up. Straighten both legs toward the ceiling in an open V-position. 1
> Inhale again with a stable powerhouse, and focus your eyes on your belly button. Press your navel down deeper into your spine. 2
> Roll back just as far as the bottom of your shoulder blades, keeping your head and neck lifted. 3
> As you inhale, roll back again chest first. Keep your arms and legs extended, your belly scooped, the shoulders integrated.
> Lean back until you are balancing on your tailbone, and try to hold this position for two or three seconds.

> Keep your legs outstretched in the air, and hold your ankles at all times.
> Initiate the next rocking movement by pressing your navel down into your spine again thus shifting your body gravity to the back.

Note: Keeping your shoulders stable and your arms and legs straight helps stabilize the torso.

Do not roll back onto the back of your neck. If you find it difficult to keep your balance with extended legs, grasp your legs behind your calves. To achieve a true rolling movement, pull in your abdominals to initiate the rocking-back movement. You tend to lose your arched back and the movement is jerky if you throw your head and shoulders back.

1

2

3 5 times

101

Repeat each side 4 times alternating

A stronger back, tighter buttocks

Single leg kicks

The "Single leg kicks" is an excellent exercise used to stabilize the hips and to give you a good strong feeling in the shoulders. It works and strengthens the buttocks, back and shoulders, stretches the front of the thighs and enhances straight posture.

> Lie on your stomach. Prop yourself up on your elbows, form a wide V-position with your arms and clasp your hands together. Extend your legs out long. Pull your navel up into your spine while pressing your elbows firmly down into the mat so that your neck is long and your spine "lifts" slightly. In the meantime focus your eyes on your hands.

> As you exhale, activate your power-house.
> Bend your right knee, and kick your right heel to your right buttock with three light but precise "beats". Keep your spine long and hips stable. The beats feel as if you were pressing down on a balloon.

Note: Pay close attention to your torso. Do not sink and hang into your shoulders like a hammock, but rather press your shoulders down creating space between your shoulder blades. Keep your neck long. Keep the hip of the kicking leg stable!

Double heel kicks

Be careful with your lower back when doing the "Double heel kicks". Work with minimum effort!
This exercise works and strengthens the entire back, especially the midback and back muscles, as well as buttocks, legs and chest muscles.

> Lie on your stomach. Rest your right cheek on a folded towel. Extend your legs and clasp your hands behind you placing them as high up on your back as possible.

> As you exhale, activate your powerhouse, bend your knees, and give three light but pressured kicks to your buttocks. Keep your pubic bone stable. **2**

> With your powerhouse secure, extend your legs back down to the mat, and stretch your arms back to follow them so that both arms and legs are stretched, and bring your upper back off the mat in an arched position. **3**

> Hold your breath and return your head and upper body to the mat, turning your face to the other side.

Note: Your pubic bone remains firmly on the mat.

2

3 Each side 3 times alternating

Swimming

The "Swimming" exercise incorporates the individual components of "The star" modifications (p. 76–77) making the exercise more difficult, but it strengthens the muscles along your spine, the abdominals and especially the stabilizer muscles.

> Lie on your stomach and completely extend your arms and legs.

> Inhale, and reach for the wall in front of you with your fingertips.

> Activate your powerhouse. Pull back your shoulder blades, press down lightly onto your extended feet stretching your knees, and simultaneously lift your arms, legs and head a few inches off the mat. Keep your neck long focusing your eyes on the floor in front of you.

> Keep your arms and legs outstretched during the exercise, and swim with your arms and legs alternately and precisely. Keep your belly scooped, your shoulders down and far away from your ears and your torso stable.

> Count backwards from five during the swimming, and then release.

Note: Keep your hips as perfectly still as possible and your legs extended. Do not swim from your knees. Keep your shoulders stable and at a maximum distance from your ears!

1   2 times

The spine twist

"The spine twist" straightens the spine while simultaneously performing the twisting movement. It is a good exercise to stabilize the hips and enhance straight posture.

> Sit up very tall. Straighten your legs out in front of you, your heels pressing out from under you, the buttocks and feet pressing into the mat beneath you. Stretch your arms out to both sides at shoulder level so that you can see your hands from the corners of your eyes. Make your neck long and relaxed. Imagine your spine is tied to the ceiling on imaginary puppet strings.

> As you exhale, activate your power-house, and then twist your torso to the right. The shoulders turn to the right, then your chest and torso. Only twist as far as your hips can remain firm and stable. 2

> Keep this position, inhale deeply, and then exhale.

Note: Make sure you sit up straight and tall, and imagine your body is a screw which is being pulled out of a socket. Keep your hips stable, your shoulders pressing down and your arms out-stretched.

If you are sitting with your legs straight "behind" your buttocks, your spine is arched and you are cramped in the groin, pull your heels up a bit toward you, bending your knees. Then do the exercise with knees bent.

Balancing your body

Teaser

Here is the original "hard nut". It requires a very stable torso and is a challenge for the entire body. People with back problems or a very defined hollow back should approach this exercise with caution.

> Start in the neutral position. Stretch your arms long by your sides, lift your legs, and bend your knees. **1**
> Inhale. As you exhale, activate your powerhouse. Stretch your legs out sinking your spine into the mat beneath you, and then lower your legs a few inches. **2**
> Keep your powerhouse stable, stretch out your hands, lift your head bringing your chin to your chest, reach for your toes, and roll up your spine to a stable position so that both arms and legs form a V-position.
> Pull your navel back into your spine, your shoulders are integrated, your neck long, the spine slightly arched and your legs extended. Focus your eyes on your feet. **3**
> Hold this position for one or two seconds, and then release, rolling your spine back down into the mat and lowering your legs.

Note: Keep your shoulders as relaxed as possible and pressed down and away from your ears.

Make sure your spine is arched. This helps you keep your position. Try to maintain the feeling of your spine pressing into the mat even if your spine is arched.

Modification: All fours

If you have mastered the first version, you can then go ahead:

> Start in the neutral position. Your arms and legs are stretched down and out.
> As you exhale, stabilize, and lift your legs, arms and head at the same time forming a V-position.

IMPORTANT

A RELAXED NECK – STRONG ABDOMINALS

If you still feel tension in your neck during the abdominals exercises, go back to the easier basic exercise to strenghten your stabilizer muscles again ("Curl-ups", p. 58, "Side curl-ups", p. 59, "Nose circles" p. 60).

1

2

3 4 times

A slim waist, healthy hips

The side kick series

"The side kick series" works your entire torso and tones the legs and waistline. It also gives you a feeling of how to develop straight posture even in a horizontal position.

> Lie on your side stretching your lower arm above your head. Place a folded towel between your arm and head. Place your top hand pressing down into the mat in front of you and your shoulders pressing down and away from your ears. Extend your legs, but do not align them with your spine, put them at a thirty-degree angle instead. Keep your knees together, raise your lower back (test this position by pushing your top arm between your waist and the mat). 1

> As you exhale, activate your powerhouse, and lift your top leg parallel to the floor. Keep your navel pulled back into your spine and your shoulders pressed down and away from your ears. 2

> Swing your extended leg and heel forward, parallel to the floor, keeping your torso perfectly stable. 3

> Stretch your toes and swing your leg back keeping your torso stable and relaxed.

Note: Make sure your leg remains in the horizontal position when swinging back and forth. You tend to drop your leg forward and raise it when swinging back. Keep your torso stable and aligned. It is so easy to "lean on" your upper body when rocking back and forth.

Keep your leg extended, and make sure your hips do not rock back and forth as you proceed.

Modification: Leg circles

> As you exhale, activate your power-house, and lift your top left leg until it is parallel to the mat.

> Keep your torso stable, continue breathing, and draw circles in the air with your extended leg.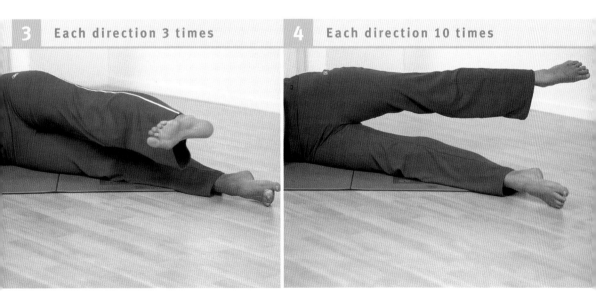

HIPS FORWARD

TIP

Roll your top hip slightly forward, and then do the exercise. Is it more intense? More effective? Then you are doing it correctly!

Note: Do not let your top hip roll back, but keep your hips even and together.

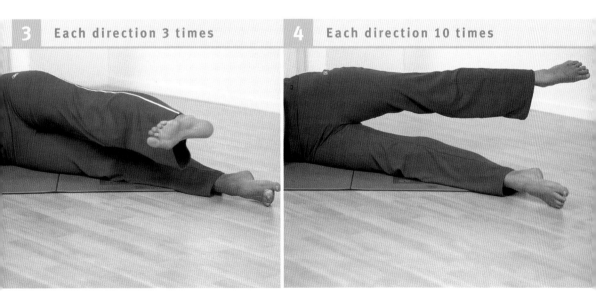

3   Each direction 3 times   **4**   Each direction 10 times

The shoulder bridge

"The shoulder bridge" is an exercise demanding very exact movements. It strengthens the buttocks and thighs, stabilizes the torso and mobilizes the spine. Go back and take another look at the preparation for the "Shoulder Bridge" on p. 84.

> Go into the neutral position. Place your hands on your hips.

> As you exhale, activate your power-house by squeezing your buttocks together. Pull your navel deep into your spine, and then roll your spine into the mat. Raise your hips, and roll each vertebra as far as the center of your chest. **1**

> Place your weight onto your left foot, and stretch your right leg out long flexing your foot at the height of your knees. **2**

> Inhale, raise the extended leg and foot up to the ceiling. **3**

> Exhale, and lower your extended leg and foot back to knee level.

> Repeat the lifting-lowering movement again.

> Do the exercise slowly and precisely, breathe deeply. Press your shoulders down into the mat staying lifted in your hips. Your belly is scooped.

> Then lower your foot slowly and con-trolled, and roll back each vertebra of your spine.

> Then change legs.

Note: Do not tense up your shoulders! Do not allow your hips to "drop" during the exercise. Press the supporting leg into the mat using your hands to help control this position.

Roll your spine down correctly!

TIP

STRETCHING FOR A CHANGE

"The shoulder bridge" puts a lot of strain on the back of the thighs. Grant your legs a bit of stretching afterward (p. 54–55).

If your hips still tend to drop or tip over, go back to the exercises "Shoulder bridge: Preparation" (p. 84) or to "The oyster" (p. 65). Both of these exercises stimulate your hip stabilizer muscles.

1

2

3   2 times | 3 sets

A supple spine

Mermaid

The "Mermaid" is a wonderful exercise used to stretch your waistline. Unfortunately, it is not suitable for people with severe knee problems.

> Sit up tall to one side with your knees slightly bent and together. Grab your left ankle with your left hand.
> Inhale. Raise your right arm to the ceiling, activate your powerhouse, and lift up your right arm in a smooth flowing motion directly alongside your left ear, stretching overhead so that you feel a light stretch. **1**
> Continue breathing, and stretch a bit more when exhaling by taking hold of your ankle with your top hand and bringing your supporting arm "overhead".
> Return to the starting position.
> Now place your right hand on the mat slightly away from your hips. The left hand floats to the ceiling. **2**
> Place your weight on your right arm, and increase the stretch to the right until your right lower arm is lying on the mat, and you feel a slight stretch in the left side of your chest. **3**
> Hold this position for a moment.

1

> Press down on your right hand stretching out your arm again, and return to the starting position.
> Repeat the stretching movements, and then change sides. Your belly is scooped, your neck long and your

2

3   Repeat each side twice

shoulders are pressing down and out
during the entire exercise.
Note: Make sure your shoulders do not
slide up to your ears during the exercise.
Try to imagine yourself being suspended
at your hips by a thick rubber band. Be

careful in the second part of the
exercise: You tend to "drop" your head
to your shoulder when pressing down
onto your right lower arm.

Strong shoulders, firm hips

Leg pull-down

The "Leg pull-down" strengthens the powerhouse as well as the hip and shoulder stabilizer muscles; a good exercise for your calves. Photos 1–4 show a sequence of movements. Go back again and recall the preparation exercise on p. 83.

> Get down on all fours. Place your arms onto the mat beneath your shoulders, spread your legs slightly apart. Stretch your neck and lengthen your spine.
> Press down slightly onto the heels of your hands stretching your arms and neck and lifting your spine. **1**

> Inhale, and as you exhale, activate your powerhouse.
> Press the back of your right foot gently into the mat, pushing it back and out until your leg is extended, and you can press yourself up onto the balls of your feet. **2**
> Keep your powerhouse stable, and do the same with your left leg, pressing yourself up into a push-up position. Your powerhouse is active, the shoulders integrated and the hips aligned with the shoulder and ankles. **3**

> Inhale as you lift your right leg a few inches straight off the mat. Keep your belly scooped and your body weight centered, keeping your spine and neck long.

> Exhale, and push your left heel back.

> Inhale, bring your left leg back, and put down your right foot.

Note: Make sure to keep your hips aligned with your feet and head, and that you squeeze your buttocks tightly. Press your shoulders down and out, and place your spine firmly between your shoulders. Do not allow your spine to hang down.

Press the heels of your hands into the mat, and stretch your neck to the ceiling to avoid it hanging down. If you find there is too much pressure on your wrists, push them forward a bit or shift your body weight to the back.

3

4   Repeat each side 3 times

Exercise program

The following three exercise programs show you how different and diversified Pilates training is. Enjoy a relaxed workout, work on feminine problem areas, or strengthen your back ligaments with the back workout!

Relaxation workout

Leave the daily stress behind you!

Time: Approx. 20 minutes

1. **Breathing through your chest** (p. 44)
2. **Activating the hips** (p. 45)
3. **Small knee circles** (p. 48)
4. **Hip rolls** (p. 52)
5. **Torpedo** (p. 85)
6. **Arms open** (p. 49)
7. **Lengthening the neck** (p. 62)
8. **The bundle** (p. 77)
9. **The roll-down** (p. 70)
10. **Rolling like a ball** (p. 86–87)
11. **Pillow press** (p. 64)
12. **Shinbone press** (p. 47)
13. **Nose circles** (p. 60)
14. **Hip muscle stretch** (p. 56)
15. **Back muscle stretch** (p. 57)
16. **The wheel** (p. 67)

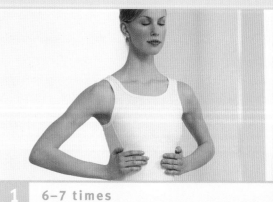

1 6–7 times

5 Each side 4 times

9 4 times

13 Circle 5–10 times

| **2** | 5 times | **3** | Each side 3 times | **4** | Each side 3–4 times |

| **6** | Each side 3 times | **7** | 6–7 times | **8** | Repeat once |

| **10** | 5 times | **11** | 5 times | **12** | 3–4 times |

| **14** | Each side once | **15** | Repeat once | **16** | 4 times |

Abdominals-thighs-buttocks workout:

This is a workout for female problem areas that strengthens the muscles and tones the curves. Time: Approx. 35 to 40 minutes.

1   5 times

5   4 sets

9   3 times in each direction

13   Each side 6 times

2   6–7 times   **3**   Each side 5 times   **4**   Each side 5 times

6   5 times   **7**   3 sets of 10 beats   **8**   Each side twice

10   5 times   **11**   3 times   **12**   Each side once

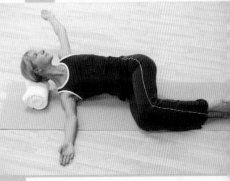

14   5–10 times   **15**   Each side twice   **16**   Each side twice

Workout for a healthy back

This is a workout that strengthens the back muscles and prevents pain.
Time: Approx. 30 minutes

1 **Activating the powerhouse** (p. 46–47)

2 **Chalk circles** (p. 69)

3 **Hip rolls** (p. 52)

4 **Curl-ups** (p. 58)

5 **Side curl-ups** (p. 59)

6 **Hip muscle stretch** (p. 56)

7 **Back muscle stretch** (p. 57)

8 **Rolling up the spine** (p. 52–53)

9 **Stretching the back of the thighs** (p. 54–55)

10 **Lengthening the neck** (p. 62)

11 **The bundle** (p. 77)

12 **The Cat** (p. 80)

13 **The eye of the needle** (p. 81)

14 **Neck stretch** (p. 66)

15 **Roll-downs** (p. 70)

16 **Rolling like a ball** (p. 86–87)

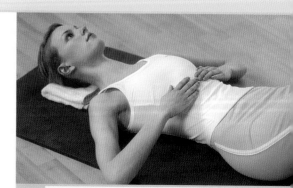

1 6–7 times

5 Each side 5 times

9 Each side once

13 Each side 3 times

2	Each side twice	**3**	Each side 3–4 times	**4**	Each side 5 times
6	Each side once	**7**	Repeat once	**8**	5 times
10	6–7 times	**11**	Repeat once	**12**	5 times
14	Each side once	**15**	4 times	**16**	5 times

Index

Index of exercises

The most important
points at a glance

JUST EVERY LEVEL OF RELAXATION!

The Pilates training program helps to make you aware of how to relax your body, making it easier and faster to get started into the day. You will become more aware of the physical shape and condition you are in, and you will learn to release and reduce tension and pressure during training and in your daily life!

HOW DO YOU SAY THE NAME?

Joseph Pilates, the man who developed the Pilates training program, was German, and that is why his name is literally pro-nounced Pi-la-tes. Only in English-speaking countries is the "e" replaced by a long "i", thus Pi-la-tiis.

Go barefoot and be comfortable

It's very important that you feel comfortable in your workout clothes, and so choosing your workout clothes depends on just how you feel in them. Especially make sure that the pants give you unlimited freedom of movement. Just lie on the floor and pull your leg up toward you and test to see if the pants tug and pull in the crotch. A super sensation: Do the Pilates training program barefoot, but you can put on socks, if you like.

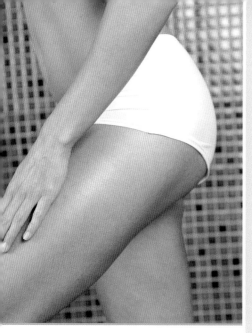

Say goodbye to problem areas!

Who doesn't want to do a workout that tones, tightens and strengthens your abdominal, chest, and buttock muscles. Pilates helps you work on your problem areas effectively, exactly, and with visible results. It is important to strengthen your body uniformly and symmetrically, incorporating the exercises for your back muscles and not just concentrating on your abdominals. Your reward is an overall shaped, toned, healthy and beautiful body that is just as balanced out and refreshed as your mind and soul!

THE BUNDLE!

"The Bundle" is an exercise that is an absolute must to strengthen your back after finishing your training program. Your back just loves and needs to arch! And this is how it goes: Get into a crouched position by sitting up on your heels and place the upper part of your body on your thighs – and just enjoy this relaxing moment for your back! Just great ...

A STRONG BODY CORE

Working with the powerhouse was the be all and end all of the training method for Joseph Pilates. Why? Because strengthening the low-lying abdominal and back muscles has a positive and relaxing effect on the muscle tone of the entire body. During the workout, pay special close attention to activating your powerhouse with the energy from within. Your body will really appreciate it!

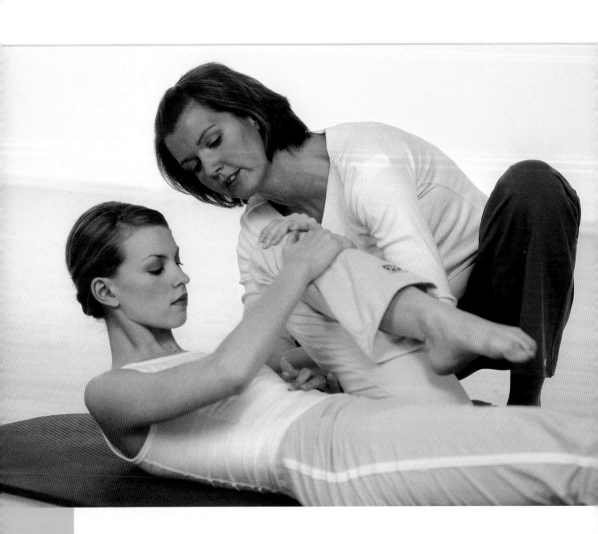

THE AUTHOR

Antje Korte is an educator and Pilates trainer and has many years of experience in physical training. She studied modern and classical dance and jazz in Düsseldorf and New York, and during one of her longer stays in New York she got to know and love Pilates. She completed her instruction as a Pilates trainer at Body Control Pilates in London and was instructed and trained on the special equipment in the Center Circle Pilates Studio in Munich, Germany. Antje Korte has her own studio on the Lower Rhine, where she teaches matwork classes as well as works with the special Pilates equipment as a personal trainer. She is a member of Body Control Pilates in London and the Pilates Method Alliance, Florida.